CAREER ELEVATOR
A Graduate Roadmap to

Getting Hired, Promoted, and Creating Your Dream Job

Fiona McKeon

Forward by Tim Draper

For more information, email mckeon.fiona@gmail.com

ISBN:

E Book – 978-1-7398978-0-2

Paperback - 978-1-7398978-1-9

GET YOUR FREE GIFT!

To enhance the experience with this book, readers who download and use our free Future MBA *You're Hired* board game can share some of the tips from this book with others.

We took the liberty of adapting the term MBA to heighten the learning experience through games:

M Making

B Business

A An Adventure

You can get a copy by visiting:
http://www.careerelevatorbook.com/freeboardgame

Why Play Board Games?

Have fun with friends and family!

Share in an educational or training setting!

- Experience hands-on learning
- Actively participate in learning
- Practical application of curriculum
- Reinforcement of terminology
- Promotes communication and collaboration
- Develops tolerance and negotiation skills
- Introduces new knowledge

To my family,
you know how much you all mean to me.

Foreword

Career Elevator is a unique book that takes you through the soft skills needed to advance in your career.

So many times, I have been in a tough spot and at the mercy of someone or another, and I know that the outcome will be determined by both what I say and how I say it. For example, when a policeman pulls me over and asks, "Do you know how fast you were going?" I respond, "Yes, officer, eighty-two miles per hour." Then he asks, "Are you in a hurry?" And I respond, "No." And he asks, "Do you know what the speed limit here is?" And I respond, "Yes, it is sixty-five."

A policeman wants the facts and as much honesty as possible. He wants the proper respect he is due for taking on the job of keeping the peace. If he detects dishonesty, he will cite you the full amount for speeding, make you appear in court, and look for other things to cite you for like not using a turn signal to pull over, an expired license plate, or anything else he can find. If he feels respect and honesty, he might lessen the citation or let you go with a warning.

Soft skills are the ability to put yourself in the shoes of the person you are dealing with. It is the ability to read if a bored employee at the DMV is trying to end their day early and you are keeping them from the door, or to understand that a person at an airline ticket counter is frazzled by the rash of people in line complaining about the canceled flight. Is the crabby hostess at a restaurant angry at a man for trying to ask her on a date while she is working? Whatever is going on in someone's mind, it is your mission to try to know it, understand it, and manage your interaction with that person appropriately to the situation.

Each situation requires a different approach and each person is different.

Thousands of entrepreneurs come to my office to pitch me each year, hoping I will invest in their companies. They often are nervous and stutter and sweat when they meet me. Sometimes they become tongue-tied. Sometimes, they just put on a show where they try to be something that they are not. Often, they are unprepared and try to wing it. I try to assuage the situation to get the best I can out of each entrepreneur who comes in. I don't want the nerves, the show, or the lack of preparation to dictate the outcome of the pitch. I want to meet the real person. So, I work with them.

I don't usually let them speak for more than a few minutes before I rattle them with questions. I try to get them to level with me about the current state of the business. I work with them to trust me to keep their information confidential, so I can get the whole picture before I make a decision.

I also want them to see me as a person rather than just a wad of money they are angling to get invested in their company. I try to tell them something personal, if I have time, to get them to a human connection.

And when I pitch my fund to a potential LP investor, I try to do the same thing. The person comes first. In many cases, the first person I talk to doesn't have decision-making authority, or at least not full authority, so it needs to be a soft sell. I want that person to want to work with me to pitch the rest of the decision makers to come to the right conclusion. I recognize that it is not just the money, it is the fit that matters.

Everyone I meet has a trust switch, the switch that opens them up and shows the real true beautiful person under the armored exterior.

The fun and the mystery is finding what that switch is, so you can see the real person. Soft skills are critical to understanding people, their motivations, their aspirations, and their dreams.

I am thrilled that a book like this exists. I encourage you to dig in and unlock the people around you.

Tim Draper

Founder: Draper Associates and DFJ. Founder Draper Venture Network. Global VC.

Author of *How to be The Startup Hero*.

Original Innovation: Viral Marketing.

Venture Successes: Skype, Baidu, Tesla, Overture, PTC, Hotmail, Twitch, Robinhood, Carta, Coinbase

Founder: Draper University of Heroes, leading 5-week program for entrepreneurs.

Education: BS in Electrical Engineering from Stanford. MBA from Harvard Business School

Awards: WEF's "Entrepreneur for the World, Commonwealth Club's "Distinguished Citizen," Independent Institute's "Toqueville Liberty Award," Forbes' "Midas List." Worth's "100 Most Powerful People in Finance." Top 100 most influential Harvard Alumni. AlwaysON's #1 Networked Venture Capitalist. Founded Draper Associates, DFJ, and the Draper Venture Network, a global network of venture capital funds. He funded Baidu, Tesla, Skype, SpaceX, Twitch, Hotmail, Focus Media, Robinhood, Athenahealth, Box, Cruise Automation, Carta, Planet, PTC, and fifteen other unicorns at the seed stage.

Table of Contents

Introduction

There are three things I discovered while being CEO of BizWorld Ireland, a non-profit organization, that changed my way of thinking, teaching, and learning about business.

1. Whether training young corporate professionals or teaching business basics to school pupils, I was struck by how important it was for the students to learn and develop soft skills. We had thought that we just needed to teach the mechanics of starting a business, essentially the hard skills.

2. The class teachers also noticed this and saw their pupils grow in confidence and resilience as they learned about business. They admitted that they didn't have time and there was no room on a busy curriculum for teaching all of these soft skills.

3. Highly qualified and motivated corporate people realized that they were well equipped with the hard skills for a career in business but that they had to learn the soft skills themselves or on the job. They wished that they had learned more communication, team building, negotiation, resilience, self-awareness, empathy, confidence, and presentation skills in school.

I thought that the tough game of business was all about hard skills. Now I realize that soft skills are essential in business and can even be more important.

Career Elevator **was born out of this revelation.**

Having taught, lectured, and mentored students of all ages, I have seen the importance of learning soft skills for personal and professional development. I have trained the staff of large corporate businesses and in the hospitality industry and witnessed how people of any age can benefit and grow from nurturing their soft skills.

I was lucky enough to be CEO of BizWorld Ireland for over a decade. BizWorld is a not-for-profit organization teaching business skills to pupils in schools worldwide. In Ireland, we worked with corporate partners to teach business as a complementary discovery learning workshop in schools.

Through this very rewarding and enlightening role, I have learned that soft skills are essential for business—and for life.

Whether you want to be a better communicator, make a good impression, be successful at an interview, or go beyond this and be promoted to the next level, you can master the soft skills needed for success through the *Career Elevator*.

Career Elevator is a complementary guide to any curriculum or graduate's educational program. Through quizzes, checklists, acronyms, activities, top tips, and a free downloadable board game, you will learn what they couldn't always teach you in school.Not these quizzes and games will equip the next generation with the skills needed to:

1. Get *into* business,

2. Get *on* in business, and maybe even

3. Get *started* on their own business.

"Education is a social process. Education is growth. Education is not a preparation for life; education is life itself."

John Dewey

How to make the *Career Elevator* work for you.

The book is divided into three parts:

Part One: You're Hired

Part Two: To Promotion and Beyond

Part Three: I'm an Entrepreneur, Now What?

A quick overview of the learning looks like this:

You're Hired	**To Promotion and Beyond**	**I'm an Entrepreneur, Now What?**
All About You	All about communicating with others	All about you as an entrepreneur
All About the Interviews	All about Etiquette	All about you starting a business
All About Your Next Steps to success	All about communicating in public	All about pitching your business and leading a team

Each part will teach you the steps needed to develop and hone your soft skills, whether you are going to be working on your own or as part of a team. This book is for you if you want to lead, make a difference at work or school, enhance your potential, or sharpen your professional image.

Even if you are already working, there may be gaps in your professional and personal development that you can fill through this book. I have structured the book so that you can revisit sections, dip into which area you want to learn, and there's even a summary I call "**The Least You Need to Know**" when you need a refresher.

Career Elevator is not rocket science, but you will learn a lot. You will learn to appreciate how important and significant it is to take care of the small things. Essentially, this program brings it all back to basics.

It is all about you and your potential!

I want people to grow professionally and unlock their potential. This is the time to invest in You. This is the time to Be Inspired, Be Inspirational, and Be Influential.

"Everybody is a genius, but if you judge a fish by its ability to climb a tree, it will live its whole life believing that it is stupid."

Albert Einstein

You've opened the book and are reading, so you must be interested or even a little bit curious. I guarantee you'll enjoy reading and learning from this book. Don't take yourself too seriously. Have a bit of fun while learning.

Let's go! Your future is in your hands!

PART ONE: YOU'RE HIRED

Featuring:

Section A: All About You

Section B: All About the Interview

Section C: All About Your Next Steps to Success

Section A:

All About You

This is where you really find out who you are and how important it is to know yourself. Having self-awareness about your personality and your talents will help you in all areas of your life. Throughout this book, I will make three promises to you:

- **Promise 1:**

The more you know about yourself, the easier it is to sell yourself to others.

- **Promise 2:**

The more you know about yourself, the easier it is to establish future goals for yourself.

- **Promise 3:**

Ultimately having more knowledge about yourself will equip you to answer the dreaded question everyone fears, "So, tell me about yourself?"

And that's how you will make a killer first impression!

Hard skills are taught in school, but soft skills are people skills and are a vital ingredient for success. These can be learned at any age. We are all born with an instinct to learn, and lifelong learning requires action. And to develop and nurture these skills, all that's required is practice.

"Education is not the filling of a pail, it's the lighting of a fire."

W.B. Yeats

In a busy school curriculum, pupils can become almost anonymous, another pail to fill. You need to know what makes you unique and how to learn more about yourself and your strengths. Your natural inquiring mind's creativity can be taught out of you, suppressed, or just not considered important enough. You may have experienced this if you have ever shared your big dreams with others and didn't receive a positive response.

The first five chapters are all about you. The next three chapters are all about the interview. The last three chapters are all about your next steps on your journey through the *Career Elevator* to "Promotion and Beyond."

Chapter 1:

What's Your X-Factor?

"One important key to success is self-confidence. An important key to self-confidence is preparation."

Arthur Ashe

To stand out from the crowd you need to make yourself known through your CV or resumé. This is the secret sauce—your X-Factor—the thing that makes you unique to everyone else with the same qualifications as you. That means getting to know what makes you unique.

What's your Unique Selling Point (USP)? Your CV and resumé must sell you to the gatekeepers in human resources. You are comfortable with your hard skills: your qualifications, education, and knowledge in the field. But what soft skills do you have and what more soft skills could you cultivate? Most other applicants will have similar qualifications to you. Make sure your resumé or application sets you apart from the others and reflects your USP.

The Least You Need to Know

Ask yourself these questions:

- What are your hobbies and interests?
- What are your strengths and talents?
- What have you achieved?
- What are you passionate about?
- What do you want to do or be?
- Where do you see yourself in one, two, five, ten years?
- Is there anything stopping you?

Don't worry if you couldn't think of answers yet. To help you do this, a **SWOT analysis** will come in handy. A SWOT analysis is used frequently in business and will be mentioned a few times in this book. It is a great tool to analyze any situation or help you make better decisions in all areas of your life.

SWOT stands for:

Strengths

Weaknesses

Opportunities

Threats

This exercise helps you break down a topic or problem into compartments. Look at the grid below. On the left side of the analysis grid are your own internal factors. The right side of the grid is concerned with external factors. You can create your own lists and answer the questions above to learn more about yourself.

Fill in the SWOT Analysis below.

Internal Factors	**External Factors**
Strengths What I am good at. What I have achieved. Not just sport and talents. What do people ask you about? What topics do you find yourself easily able to talk about?	**Opportunities** What is clearly possible ahead for you.
Weaknesses What gaps are in your strengths? What new strength or talent might be worth having?	**Threats** What is holding you back? Other than you!

Get to like and admire yourself. If you don't, no one else will. We all need to take an inventory like this and realize what we are good at. You're not too bad at all. You're quite good and you I bet you found more strengths and opportunities than you thought you had!

"The person born with a talent they are meant to use will find their greatest happiness in using it."

Johann Wolfgang von Goethe

Summary

In this chapter, you learned more about yourself.

- Your USP (Unique Selling Point)
- Your inner Strengths
- Your inner Weaknesses
- Your external Opportunities
- Your external Threats

Next Steps?

So, now that you know more about yourself, where are you going? Goals can point us in the right direction.

Chapter 2:

You and Your Goals

The more you know about your own strengths and weaknesses, the easier it will be to establish goals. What makes you stand out from others? What is your USP? The more you know about other external factors and their effect on you, the easier it will be to achieve your goals.

Goal setting requires belief in yourself and the motivation to act on these goals. You don't have to write down any goals yet. It might be too soon. Take your time. Open your mind as ideas can come to you when you're least expecting them. Use your imagination and think big. This is a private journey, so no one needs to hear what you're thinking. Don't be afraid to be ambitious. Let your mind take you one step out of your comfort zone.

Goals give us a purpose and something to strive for. Be clear about your goals. Goals work best when you write them down. You can break down your ultimate goal into smaller, achievable steps and actions that can be accomplished relatively quickly with ambition and confidence. The more well-defined your goals are, the easier it will be to achieve them.

The Least You Need to Know

Ask yourself the following: Are your goals SMART? SMART is an acronym to help you remember the five things you need to keep in mind when you are setting your goals.

- **Specific**—Focus on the outcome and try to make your goals clear.
- **Measurable**—How will you know if you have achieved them? How do you measure your progress?
- **Achievable**—Let's be realistic here! Don't set yourself up for failure.
- **Relevant**—As long as they don't require you to become an astronaut overnight, they are relevant.
- **Time-bound**—Goals can't be achieved today or tomorrow but they do have to have an end day in sight. Give yourself a realistic deadline to accomplish your goal.

Now, write some goals for yourself. Make sure that they are SMART and have some short-term and some long-term goals. Remember, they are not written in stone. You can keep changing them as you progress. That's OK. As a teacher, it took me a while to see the value of crumpled pieces of paper in a bin. Reworking and revising on paper over and over is a valuable exercise. It shows that you're thinking, you're learning, and that you're active in the process of targeting what you want to say or accomplish. Are you getting nervous? Just remember that our goals sometimes change or adapt to external situations beyond our control. Nevertheless, list your goals for now and you can always add more goals after you read the other chapters and find out more about yourself.

Be clear about your goals. Avoid confusion. Make sure that you have well-defined goals and write them down. When we write things down, we are far more likely to remember them and take them seriously. The act of writing helps your brain process and retain the information. That is why students favor writing out their notes on paper. Even young school children are encouraged to learn to trace the correct formation of letters of the alphabet in the sand and on their desks before taking up their pencils.

Imagine the possible, not the impossible. We have all read and heard about the laws of attraction and the power of positive thinking. Visualize your goals and visualize your success in achieving these. Imagine yourself lifting up that trophy or achieving your dream job.

Don't worry if some of your goals are very ambitious. Step out of your comfort zone and realize that failure is OK. So many people are reluctant to "have a go" and this form of risk aversion can be educated into us, while creativity and possibility can be educated out.

List Your Goals Again and Categorize Them as Follows:

Immediate Short-term Long-term

Then divide them into the following categories:

Achievable Ambitious

Time for a second SWOT analysis. This time taking a closer look at your goals. You can do this analysis for each goal. It will help you fine-tune your goals and even think of more goals.

Fill in the SWOT analysis of your goals.

Strengths Attributes that will help you to achieve or improve your goals.	**Opportunities** Conditions or resources which could be used to help you achieve the goals.
Weaknesses Attributes that might cause problems/harm the quality/prevent the goals from being achieved.	**Threats** Events or conditions which could restrict the achievement of the goals.

Congratulations! You have filled out two SWOT analysis grids and you've written down a few personal goals. Reward yourself. It is very difficult to spend so much time thinking and writing about yourself. You have taken the first step on your *Career Elevator* journey. It should become clearer now, how your goals can be made possible whether they be short-term or long-term; achievable or ambitious.

You can go back and rewrite your goals anytime. Remember, they're not anyone else's goals, they're yours. Hopefully, your mind has begun to open and question things. Something as simple as a SWOT analysis can really clarify what you are trying to accomplish. Keep on thinking and questioning. Ask yourself questions about where you're going and what you want to achieve. Write them in this book or put them in a notebook.

"Learn from yesterday, live for today, hope for tomorrow. The important thing is to not stop questioning."

Albert Einstein

Summary

In this chapter, we learned more about where you are going. Your goals must be SMART.

- **S** Specific
- **M** Measurable
- **A** Achievable
- **R** Relevant
- **T** Time-bound

Next Steps?

What is the most difficult question people of all ages dread being asked?

Read on to find out what it is and how to answer it.

Chapter 3:

Know Your Personal Elevator Pitch

All people, no matter what age or how successful, dread the following question: "Tell me about yourself?" It sounds simple, doesn't it? But it certainly puts everyone on the spot as you try to answer such a broad question in a coherent way. You must be able to answer this question clearly in approximately thirty to sixty seconds.

I usually get people to introduce themselves at my classes and courses and have honestly been taken aback at how nervous grown adults are when posed this question. We will be covering mastering the art and nerves of public speaking in Part Two ("To Promotion and Beyond"), but for now, let's concentrate on the short statement that you will need to make over and over as you journey through life.

This is called your personal elevator pitch, and everyone needs one. Whether you're in school, college, or in the workforce, you need to be able to answer that question clearly and concisely. Remembering your elevator pitch is as simple as looking at the palm of your hand. It's that easy. I promise you.

"Practice isn't the thing you do once you're good. It's the thing you do that makes you good."

Malcolm Gladwell

The Least You Need to Know

For now, just answer these questions briefly. We will structure it later so that you can remember it.

1. Who am I?
2. What is my educational or job experience?
3. What are my hobbies and interests?
4. What are my key strengths?
5. What are my main goals?

You can memorize the answers to these five questions to create your personal elevator pitch.

What is an Elevator Pitch?

The original term *elevator pitch* or elevator speech comes from the need for entrepreneurs to get funding for their business when the internet was born. As competition was fierce, the pitch had to be engaging from the first second and short enough to explain exactly what the person's business did in thirty seconds. In other words, the pitch had to be as concise and persuasive enough to convince an investor to invest in the short time span of an elevator ride.

An elevator pitch is like a business card or the home page of a website. We will learn more about elevator pitches for entrepreneurs in Part Three. For now, you just need a personal elevator pitch. It is essentially the answer to the frightening question: "Tell me about yourself."

To create an outline of your elevator pitch, answer the following questions which suit your audience. You may modify it slightly depending on whether you are at a job interview or at a networking event.

Be true to yourself and above all, be brief. Practice makes perfect, so learn this pitch by reciting it over and over (use your phone to record it and listen back—no doubt you will make changes).

As you can see from below, the previous chapter on goals feeds into your personal elevator pitch.

Delivering your personal elevator pitch can be nerve-wracking, so to assist you, I have devised a practical physical way to keep you focused and on track.

Give Yourself a Hand

Look at the palm of your hand. You have a thumb and four fingers. Your elevator pitch needs five points. This is a quick and easy way to remember your five points. Look below and choose the outline that best suits your current personal situation.

For Jobseekers:

1. My name is... and I'm from...
2. I am studying/I have studied/I am qualified in...
3. My favorite hobbies are...
4. My main talents/achievements are...
5. My dream job is...

For Students:

1. My name is and I live in...
2. I study at...
3. My favorite subjects are...
4. My talents/hobbies/achievements are...
5. I think I'd like to do/be... in the future

For Current Employees:

1. My name is an I work at... organization
2. I do... in my daily role
3. My main objective through this work is to...
4. My hobbies/interests are...
5. My ambition is to do... or work at...

The answers to each question give you an outline for your pitch. Expand on each answer but make sure that it is no more than ninety words long. Don't be tempted to be overly perfect as it does need to sound sincere and genuine. Write it here or in a notebook.

"When you greet people with a smile, you'll have a good time meeting them and they'll have a good time meeting you."

Dale Carnegie

Action 1: Read your elevator pitch aloud to yourself. Is it pleasant, short, and to the point?

Don't forget to smile. Yes, you can hear a smile in a voice even when you are not seeing the person.

Don't be afraid to speak slowly. Remember that you will eventually know this pitch by heart, but the person you're speaking to is hearing it for the first time. Slowly does it.

A practical way to aid you in remembering your pitch is to place your left hand by your side touching your thigh. Press each finger to your thigh as you deliver the five points of your pitch. Start with the thumb. This also serves to keep your hand quiet as when we are nervous our hands can tend to show nervousness through swinging our arms or fidgeting with our fingers.

Action 2: Record yourself delivering your elevator pitch.

My first Image Consultancy training course made me nervous as I wasn't comfortable or confident teaching adults, even though I taught kids every day. For practice, I recorded myself on my son's Fisher-Price toy tape recorder. It was red, blue, yellow, and white plastic and it had a small microphone on a coiled lead. Then I listened to my recording on the cassette as I drove my car until I was happy hearing my own voice delivering the opening lines of a speech confidently. When I was stopped at traffic lights going over and over my lines, I'm sure people in cars beside me thought I was crazy!

You won't have to speak into a toy tape recorder. We are all fortunate to have a great tool at our disposal, our smartphones. Record and listen back to hear how well you remembered your elevator pitch. This is a good test for remembering it when you meet people.

Now, listen back again to how well you delivered it. Remember, you're not in school now. It doesn't have to be right the first time. We all need practice when learning something new.

Ask yourself the following questions:

- How was this pitch?
- Did I sound pleasant?
- Did I speak clearly and slowly?

Practice your pitch over and over until you're happy with a final recorded version. With practice, it will come as naturally to you as a good habit.

Summary

In this chapter, we learned about how to deliver an elevator pitch answering the following questions:

- Who am I?
- What stage of life am I at?
- What are my skills?
- What are my goals?

Next Steps?

Now that you've recorded yourself several times, you may have noticed something.

Were your words and actions fluent? Probably not right away. The next chapter will help us bust any nervous habits.

Chapter 4:

Habit Busting

"Depending on what they are, our habits will either make us or break us. We become what we repeatedly do."

Sean Covey

Retraining our habits is a good way to get rid of annoying, distracting sounds and actions when we speak. How many times did you use "um," "eh," or "like" in your early recordings?

Using those filler words (um, eh, and like) can be a distraction for the listener. To get the most fluent and clear message across you need to eliminate these annoying sounds from your elevator pitch. It's easy to break these bad habits. It's all in your hands!

A habit is just that. Something which we repeatedly do, unconsciously or consciously. Brushing your teeth is a conscious good habit. Saying "you know," after every sentence, especially when you are nervous, is a distracting habit that undermines what you are trying to say. So, let's foster the good and minimize the not-so-good habits.

Practice makes perfect! It takes twenty-one days to form a habit to make it normal to you. It most likely takes the same number of days to discard a bad habit.

In communicating with others, a habit could be verbal, like saying "um" when you are trying to think of what to say. It could also be a visual habit, like a distracting gesture such as biting your nails or fiddling with your hair or ears.

The Least You Need to Know

How do you break a bad habit? Here is a very easy way to do so, in fact, a person made a lucrative profit through this many years ago. It was called "Snapback to Reality" or the Rubber Band Cure.

Essentially, it was the use of a rubber band on the wrist. You just wear a rubber band on your wrist (not too loose, but not tight either). Every time the person finds themselves using their bad habit, whether it's a word, an action, or even a negative thought, they were advised to pull the band and then snap it back on the wrist. That small reminder helped break the habit.

It's mind over matter. Developing a physical awareness of something that we unconsciously do. You associate that physical sensation of the rubber band with the habit.

I used a physical technique with my student teachers. As future teachers, they were becoming aware of mannerisms and certain repeated words that could distract pupils from their lessons. So, I suggested that every time they caught themselves saying or doing it, they could physically turn the face of their watch the other way, twist a ring around their finger the wrong way around, or move a bracelet to the other wrist. The idea was to do something physical every time.

You can do this to rid yourself of those distracting words that punctuate your elevator pitch. Every time you find yourself using those words or sounds in your day-to-day conversations, do something physically with an item of jewelry worn on the hand. At first, you will only catch yourself offending once or twice. However, as you increasingly switch that bracelet around or take some small physical action, you will eventually pick up and notice yourself and bad habits almost all the time.

Be patient, it does take more than two weeks, but you will know you're cured when you go to turn your item of jewelry before you even say the word.

It really works. Try it.

If you don't wear jewelry, a rubber band will work for you.

Breaking any bad verbal or physical habits will not only aid the fluency of your elevator pitch but will help you in any future conversations with people whom you want to impress.

Personal Milestone Checklist

Reward yourself. Clap yourself on the back. You really are learning new skills!

What have you done?

You know your goals. Check □

You know your USP. Check □

You know how to answer the question, "Tell me about yourself?" Check □

You can deliver your elevator pitch clearly and fluently. Check □

You know how to rid yourself of words and actions that interrupt the flow of your pitch. Check □

Summary

In this chapter, we learned about how habits can interrupt our flow when speaking.

- Repeated words like “um,” “eh,” and “like” can interrupt the fluency of our pitch.
- Repeated actions with our hands can distract from our message.
- Using an item of jewelry or a rubber band on our wrist can help us break bad habits.

Next Steps?

But how do you get to the place where someone will listen to your elevator pitch and can hear your fluent speaking voice?

Let’s learn how to make a killer first impression.

Keep going, you’re on a roll!

Chapter 5:

First Impressions Matter!

"You never get a second chance to make a first impression."
Andrew Grant

According to experts, first impressions matter and we size up new people in somewhere between thirty seconds and two minutes.

It is human nature to judge a person in a few seconds based on our senses in the following order: sight and sound. Therefore, we make judgments based on what we see first and then on what we hear.

We always tend to trust our gut instinct, so we often judge a person by the first impression they make. According to a Harvard study, it takes eight positive encounters to change a negative first impression of someone. Make your first impression a fabulous one.

During any interaction, whether it be a meeting, a presentation, or an interview, if we impress well with the combination of appropriate actions, appearance, and voice, the greater the chance that the listener will take what we say seriously.

This is according to Dr. Mehrabian's formula for communication from a 1971 study at UCLA. This study concluded that 93 percent of communication is "nonverbal" in nature. Using the data from these studies, Dr. Mehrabian devised a formula to describe how the mind determines meaning. He concluded that the interpretation of a message is 7 percent verbal, 38 percent vocal, and 55 percent visual. You can see how important it is to not only know what you are talking about, but to look the part too.

"First Impressions are turned into lasting impressions when your behavior remains consistent... you are always on stage, being observed."

Jeff Blount

The Least You Need to Know

The first impression we make is our own personal brand. Your brand is what people say and think of you professionally and personally.

To work on your personal brand, simply go back to BASICS:

B - Body language and posture: Do you stand and sit up straight?

A - Actions: Can you eliminate annoying gestures such as fiddling with your hair when speaking?

S - Social skills and handshaking: Do you know how to behave in certain situations?

I - Image management: Do you dress appropriately for certain situations?

C - Communication and facial expressions: Do you smile and speak clearly?

S - Speech: How does your voice sound when you listen to your elevator pitch?

Top Five Actions Checklist

1. Stand up straight.
2. Don't lean on anything.
3. Keep your hands out of your pockets.
4. Smile!

5. Keep good eye contact with the person you are speaking to.

Action 1: Video Yourself Delivering Your Elevator Pitch.

Look back at it. You are not concerned with the words anymore as by now they should be near perfect. Instead, focus on your body language and posture and ask yourself the following:

- Are you standing up straight?
- Are you leaning on anything?
- Are you moving or standing still?
- Are you smiling?
- Are you fiddling with anything?
- What are your hands doing?
- While looking at yourself speaking, did any of your body language distract from your pitch?

Like it or not, we are all standing, walking, talking, and sitting IMAGES. So, manage them. Our actions paint a picture of who we are and therefore give an impression of us. An impression is an image.

The following is a good statement to consider while managing your image for making a positive first impression.

I - I will

M - Manage my

A - Actions

G - Gestures

E - Etiquette

S - Style

It is definitely worth giving appropriate attention to your first impression.

Eventually, through practice, you will be making a sensational first impression. And that means success.

Summary

In this chapter, we learned the following about making a good first impression so that:

- Others will listen to us.
- Others will take us seriously.
- Others will not have to meet us repeatedly to change an initial negative impression.

Conclusion of Section 1: All About You

In order to get a job, you need to get an interview. In order to get an interview, you need to prepare a CV or resumé. To create a CV or resumé you need to know yourself. Your SWOT analysis and goals feed into the preparation of your CV or resumé.

So, when job hunting you may need to use your elevator pitch and make a good first impression even before your interview. It may be as you hand in your CV or resumé to a business or even on the telephone inquiring about a job.

Section B:

All About the Interview

"All the world's a stage."
William Shakespeare

How are you going to behave at an interview? Remember, if you made it to this point, you are being interviewed because you're qualified for the job. They already know your qualifications. Now, it's your actions that will set you apart from the other candidates. And to be honest, they will either make or break you. You are almost on stage when "performing" at an interview.

And Action!

This is the part where you learn how to stand out from the crowd. How do you differentiate yourself from every other candidate with similar qualifications and most likely similar experience? As I said before, your CV and resumé may secure you an interview, but your actions, your body language and, your voice during an interview will get you the job. How else are you going to be taken seriously?

All professional and personal interactions with people are like a brief interview or interviews. In fact, you're pitching you and yourself. Therefore, these potential interactions can and should be given as much attention and importance as the preparation for an interview. Interview skills are not only for summer jobs, but for college, apprenticeships, internships, presentations, and meetings. These are skills that will help you gain confidence in any area of your life.

"Inaction breeds doubt and fear. Action breeds confidence and courage. If you want to conquer fear do not sit at home and think about it. Go out and get busy."

Dale Carnegie

Action is all that is required to adopt, adapt, and apply learning and new skills.

Read on to learn about what actions you can take for successful interviews.

Chapter 6:

Actions—They Speak Louder Than Any Words

Our own actions speak louder than words. Even before we open our mouths, our actions at an interview can make or break us. Not paying enough attention to our actions at an interview can minimize the effect of any rehearsal and preparation in advance.

We'll talk about the power of your voice later, but what do you say when you're not speaking? Body language sends strong messages. It doesn't whisper, it screams. It is a universal language that even young children learn to read. As Dale Carnegie said, "Even before we speak, we are condemned or approved."

Your qualifications, experience, and CV/resumé will get you the interview, but your personal performance and actions at the interview will get you the job.

Top Tip 1: Wear a watch. It shows good timekeeping etiquette.

The Least You Need to Know

Interview Top 10

1. Don't be late – Know where it is and how to get there on time.
2. Be prepared – Research the company and know what it does.
3. Know your USP and your own strengths, capabilities, and experience. What's your X-Factor?
4. Rehearse and practice – Ask yourself questions you are likely to be asked.
5. Dress above the grade of the job – Remove any distracting accessories.
6. Be prepared – Consider weather with appropriate footwear and outerwear.*
7. Be professional – Have a copy of your CV/resumé with you.
8. First impressions – Smile, speak clearly, and look your interviewers in the eye.
9. Answer questions in a clear and confident manner.
10. Have your own question rehearsed to ask at the end of the interview.

*All office receptions will hold an overcoat and even a bag with different shoes for you while you present yourself for the actual interview or even a meeting with the appropriate outfit.

Top Tip 2 – Avoid being on your smartphone when anyone greets you. You have no idea if that guy on the elevator is your future manager or the owner of the company. Plus, you don't want the receptionist to report back to the interviewer that you were talking loudly on your phone or came across as rude when greeted. First impressions aren't just for the interview.

Be Prepared

Ask yourself these questions in advance of the interview and prepare credible answers.

- What are your strengths?
- Why do you want this job?
- Why do you want a new job?
- Why do you want a job with this organization? (No negativity about your current position).
- What was the hardest thing you have ever faced in your job?
- How did you resolve this? (Make sure that you did!)
- Have you real examples of your good points at work? (Stories and anecdotal references are most convincing).
- What virtues and values do you have pertaining to this new job or organization?

In addition, do not underestimate the value of any previous work experience or part-time jobs. Hobbies and interests will differentiate you from all other applicants with the same qualifications as you and give the interviewer more insight into your personality. Prepare these and make sure that they are real. You will benefit from having volunteered for an organization, even for one week. You may even be asked for the title of your favorite book. Be prepared. Don't pretend that you just read a bestseller about time management or leadership. You may get in over your head if they ask further questions about that book.

Body language speaks volumes. What we do and what we don't do tells others how we feel and could distract from what we say. Do you slouch in your chair? Do you stand tall? When you walk and do you shuffle your feet? These little things can say a whole lot about us, for good and bad.

Effective Interview Body Language

- Walk confidently into the room.
- Keep your shoulders back and head up.
- Keep hands out of your pockets.
- Shake hands confidently and firmly with your interviewers.
- Smile and look the interviewers in the eye.
- Sit comfortably but formally in the chair assigned to you, keeping both feet on the floor. Don't slouch.
- Use open hand gestures to show interest.
- Keep still. Avoid the urge to fiddle with your hands or face.
- Rest your hands with open palms gently on your thighs.
- Do not fold your arms over your chest or clench your fists or the sides of your chair.
- Sit on your hands if you can't trust them not to fidget.

How to End an Interview Positively and Confidently.

Near the end of the interview is the perfect time to ask your own questions that you have prepared. It projects confidence and lets them know that you have thought about a positive outcome from the interview. Below are some suggestions:

- When will a decision be made about the job?
- What date will the job start?
- Have you many other candidates to interview for this job?

The interviewer needs to leave with the impression that you are very interested in the position. Asking questions reinforces that. Thank your interviewers for their time at the end with a firm handshake. The following day, thank them again by email. This is an opportunity to refresh their memory of you by mentioning strong points from the interview or to address any questions that arose. Sign the email off positively expressing that you are looking forward to hearing their decision.

Top Tip 3 - Carry your laptop, bag, notebook, or papers in your left hand. This leaves your right hand free by your side and ready to shake hands when meeting someone.

Summary

In this chapter, we learned about successful actions for interviews:

- Before – Prepare
- During – Punctual, Professional, Pleasant
- After – Thank you and follow up

Next Steps?

So, you've nailed your actions for an interview. How can you make sure that the interviewers are going to listen to you? Read on to find out how important your voice is.

Chapter 7:

Great Voices Get Heard—and Taken Seriously

"Words mean more than what is set down on paper. It takes the human voice to infuse them with deeper meaning."

Maya Angelou

Listen back to your elevator pitch.

Are you happy with the quality of your voice?

People with a good, convincing voice have an easier time communicating with and persuading others. Hearing is largely considered the second strongest of the five senses. Every time you speak, the listener is subconsciously registering the quality of your voice, your pronunciation, your grammar, and your choice of words.

However, make sure to be true to who you are. Accents are charming if they're understood. It's all about your diction, which is the overall clarity of your voice and expression.

Do people hear you well? If you are having to repeat yourself often, you are either speaking too low or too fast. Make note of this and adjust your voice.

The Least You Need to Know

To sound more powerful and sincere:

- Slow down.
- Breathe calmly.
- Always maintain eye contact.
- Vary your pitch, pace, volume, and tone.
- Use pauses to help emphasize special words or phrases.

- Try to eliminate distracting filler words and sounds: “um,” and “eh,” or “like.”
- State your message clearly and avoid jargon.
- Use gestures in moderation.
- Accents are charming if they are understood.
- Improve your vocabulary.

Listen Again to the Quality of Your Voice

Your voice should be pleasant, interesting, energized, confident, and convincing.

Your voice should not be squeaky, booming, dull, monotonous, uncertain, boring, or nervous.

Below are all the aspects of our voices. Remember that practice makes perfect.

- Pace: Work at altering between speeding up, slowing down, and adding pauses.
- Volume: Aim to speak mid-range between loud and soft.
- Tone: Don't speak in a robotic monotone. Alter the tone of your voice. Smiling while you speak helps. Ask yourself what mood you want to portray.
- Pitch: Aim for halfway between a squeaky high-pitched voice and a dull low voice.
- Breathing: Avoid sounding out of breath. Get fit to generate more energy. Many of us only use 50 percent of our lung capacity. Standing tall aids the air flow to our lungs.
- Rate: Fast talkers are harder to understand than slow talkers and they frequently have to repeat themselves. Overly slow talkers make the listener impatient.
- Pronunciation: Pronounce the entire word. Don't drop final letters. For example, words ending with -ing. Always speak more slowly when on the telephone.
- Accent: Be true to yourself. If your grammar and word choice are correct, your accent can be charming. To help make your accent better understood, face the listener, and use eye contact. Keep your hands away from your face and speak at a good, average pace, but not too quickly.

As for your overall image, if your voice distracts or detracts from the main message, it is noticed immediately. This reduces the power of your message. Your voice is a significant 38 percent of your overall first impression, according to Dr. Mehrabian's study mentioned in the previous section.

Vocabulary Building

The words we use are as important as how we say them. Reading well-written news articles or books can help you expand your vocabulary. You don't want to lapse into just using corporate-speak or jargon, but it is important to round out your vocabulary with some more substantial words and phrases.

Words can also convey a sense of assuredness and confidence. Would you rather hire someone who says, "I can," or someone who says, "I guess so," and shrugs their shoulders? Using clear, direct words that imply action and accomplishment lets the interviewer know that you are a person that is ready for the position.

Try to Replace Some Less Influential Words to Make a Greater Impact.

Don't worry, it will take repeated practice, but it's good to know the difference between impressive and unimpressive words.

Influential and impressive	**Unimpressive**	**Influential and impressive**	**Unimpressive**
Will	Might	Outstanding	Good
Pivotal	Relevant	Endorsement	Agreement
However	But	Leading Edge	New
Fulfilled	Completed	Achieved	Did
We should	Perhaps we	Massive	Big
Immediately	As soon as possible	Will	Could
Global	International	Now	Soon

Summary

In this chapter, we learned about the power of your voice and its significant impact on your first impression.

- How to sound more powerful
- How to sound more sincere
- The importance of the pitch, pace, and tone of your voice
- Words that influence and those that don't

Next Steps?

So, you want to get a job. You've worked on your actions, your habits, your voice, and your vocabulary. Now for the icing on the cake: what to wear.

Chapter 8:

WWW—Working Wardrobes Work!

"Your wardrobe should complement your skill set, never detract or distract from your assets."
Nina Garcia

One of the trainees in my Image Consultancy classes agreed that feeling appropriately dressed gives you confidence. She was a part-time radio presenter, and her slots were night time. She always dressed up for her job but one night she wore a tracksuit and went to work as usual. Same time, same preparation. However, she admits that she did the worst radio show of her life that night. She just didn't feel confident in her tracksuit. She didn't feel empowered or worthy of the job and it came across in her voice. The listeners couldn't see her, but they could hear an uncertainty and lack of conviction in her voice. Making an effort and dressing professionally can boost your confidence and serve as a "suit of armor" as you engage in the highs and lows of the corporate world.

Every organization has a dress code, so it's important to investigate the organization's requirements and dress accordingly. However, dress formally at an initial interview and err on the side of caution until you have established yourself in the organization. Dressing more professionally can't hurt, but you may be remembered negatively if you show up in shorts and flip-flops or your favorite little black dress from a night out.

During meetings, interviews, and presentations, a working wardrobe gives you confidence and power. Wearing a watch also gives the impression of reliability and good timekeeping.

Accessories

They may be small things, but your accessories are also an integral part of your outfit. Make sure that you carry a good quality notebook, a nice pen (not one you buy in packs often in a convenience store) and make sure that your eyeglasses are current and up to date.

This happened to me when I was contacted by a guy who ran a great training course I attended. He said that when working with big corporations, he felt a little insecure and underconfident. I suggested that we meet for coffee to discuss, and within seconds I saw that he needed to upgrade from his dog-eared reporter's spiral-bound notebook, ditch his disposal pen, and to update his glasses. He said that those three pieces of advice made him feel as if he fitted in more in corporate environments. Small changes can have a big impact.

If people's eyes are drawn away from your face, eyes, and voice due to your clothes in any way, your power and professionalism can be undermined. They just won't listen to you or take you seriously.

The Least You Need to Know

For traditional organizations the following guidelines are appropriate. Once you know this, you can adapt to whatever industry you are working in. Keep jewelry and accessories to an appropriate standard and size. Below are some universal options that work well at almost any job interview. This is the basic "starter kit" for dressing for success.

Men

- A suit in a neutral color such as navy blue or dark gray
- A tie in a neutral color (burgundy is a color that goes well with most suit colors)
- A white or blue shirt
- Thin-soled shoes (Avoid chunky footwear at an interview)

Women

- A navy blue or dark gray skirt or trouser suit
- A silk blouse or top
- Closed-toe shoes

If you want more detailed information on what to wear to an interview, what to wear for work, and how to organize a working wardrobe, read on. Otherwise, jump straight to the next chapter.

The Most You Could Know

Working Wardrobe Top 10

1. Wear colors that mean business.
2. Wear a layer (cardigan, vest, jacket, scarf).
3. Jackets give authority.
4. Solid colors appear more professional.
5. If wearing patterns, they should only be the size of a large coin.
6. Accessories worn should be small to medium in size—aim for a quality look!
7. Smooth fabrics appear more professional.
8. Be very careful with textured fabrics.
9. Beware of showing too much skin.
10. Dress for the job you want—not the job you have!

Whether you are just entering the workforce or changing careers, organizing your closet and purging items from your wardrobe will help you stay focused and more organized. As you build that workplace wardrobe, choose classic pieces that you can mix and match and wear more than one way. Here are some top tips on how to prioritize which clothes you keep or sell.

- A working wardrobe is a wardrobe that works for you.
- We wear 20 percent of our clothes 80 percent of the time. This is The Pareto Principle, also known as the 80/20 rule.
- The most luxurious item in your wardrobe is space.
- If you can't see it, you won't wear it.
- If you can't reach it, you can't wear it.
- Get rid of clothes that you don't wear anymore. You can donate or sell on any clothes that are in good condition.
- As a result of decluttering your wardrobe, you'll be able to see everything and be able to dress more quickly in the morning.
- Keep your workwear separate from your weekend wear.

Below is a more comprehensive guide on clothing for an interview. The industry or sector that you are interviewing for will depend on how you dress for an interview. Remember, if in doubt, dress a notch above.

Interview Clothes for Men

Suits: Solid colors of dark blue or gray suggest authority and quality. It must be perfectly clean and pressed. Any stains or wrinkles will not impress.

Shirts: The simpler the better in traditional workplaces. Avoid bright colors, excessive patterns, and exaggerated cuffs.

Ties: A plain tie in a muted color plays it safe. Avoid large patterns, designer logos, or comical characters.

Socks: Best to coordinate with your suit color, making sure they are long enough not to expose bare skin when you're sitting.

Shoes: Classic laced or slip-on shoes in black or brown are most appropriate. Avoid any shiny or dress shoes and more functional shoes with thick rubber soles. Make sure that shoes are polished. Heels shouldn't be visibly worn down.

Jewelry: Less is more. Excessive jewelry can distract from you and your message.

Cologne: Less is more. Don't overpower with too much scent or use no fragrance at all.

Briefcase/Laptop bag: Make sure it is slim and clean.

Grooming: Hair, skin, and nails must be appropriate and clean.

Interview Clothes for Women

Before I address interview clothes for women, I must acknowledge that shopping and dressing for women are far more complicated and perilous simply because there is so much choice available. With more choices, there are more risks and more opportunities to make mistakes.

Keep it simple!

Skirt suit: This is a safe choice, but trouser suits are also acceptable.

Blouses/tops: Keep to a neutral color with an appropriate neckline that doesn't reveal too much.

Scarves: A scarf in an appropriate color can enhance a suit, blouse, or top.

Shoes - Avoid too high a heel. Make sure that they are in perfect condition and ideally in a color that complements your handbag is most appropriate. Avoid open-toed shoes. Tights are a must for the workplace if you are wearing a skirt.

Handbag, briefcase/laptop bag: Must be of good quality to convey authority.

Jewelry: Keep it simple. Less is more.

Perfume: Subtle. Don't overpower with too much scent or don't use fragrance if you aren't sure what is too much.

Make-up: Subtle. Keep the dramatic make-up for nights out.

Grooming: Hair, skin, and nails must be appropriate and clean.

Dress codes in the workplace can vary wildly between companies. One company's idea of casual dress may be unacceptable at another. Most of us aren't wearing a full top hat and tails as part of our job, but here is the sequence of levels of professional dress from formal to casual. You will probably find yourself landing somewhere in the middle of this list. Whatever the appropriate clothing may be, make sure your clothes are clean and not wrinkled.

Men: From Formal to Casual

1. Three-piece suit
2. Double-breasted suit
3. Two-piece suit
4. Trousers worn with a button-down shirt, tie, and a sports jacket or blazer
5. Trousers worn with a shirt and tie
6. Trousers worn with a shirt, tie, and jumper/sweater
7. Trousers teamed with shirt and jumper/sweater
8. Trousers teamed with a shirt
9. Casual trousers, casual long-sleeved shirt, and a jacket
10. Casual trousers, short-sleeved shirt
11. Jeans with shirt and jacket
12. Jeans with shirt or jumper/sweater
13. Shorts worn with a casual shirt
14. Track suit

Women: From Formal to Casual

1. Skirt suit in a matching color
2. Skirt suit that has a different colored jacket to the skirt
3. Trouser suit in a matching color
4. Jacket with trousers in a different color
5. Simple tailored dress
6. Trousers with no jacket (you lose power when you take your jacket off!)
7. Casual trousers worn with a jacket and a shirt or top
8. Casual trousers worn with a short-sleeved shirt or top
9. Jeans worn with a jacket and a shirt or top
10. Jeans worn with a shirt, top or jumper/sweater
11. Shorts worn with a casual shirt or top
12. Track suit

Grooming

Grooming is important for everyone. Make sure that hair, skin, and nails are appropriate and clean. Make sure that your breath is also clean and fresh (but don't chomp on mint gum the entire time). Cleanliness is most important but don't overpower with too much perfume or cologne. Consider limiting yourself to one set of earrings if you have multiple piercings. Cover any tattoos. The company may or may not have a policy on visible body art or piercings, but it's important to err on the side of caution in this area. Once you get the job, you will have a better sense of what is allowed or discouraged.

While you still want to express yourself and your own style, make sure you do so in a clean, presentable way. Did you spend a year growing out your beard? Make sure it is clean and tidy when you arrive. If you like bright, fun hair colors, consider styling your hair in a more subdued style. Keep the purple hair—just don't have it up in a spiky hairdo for the interview.

Rule of Thumb – The more creative the industry you work in, or interview for, the more creative your outfit can be.

Pulling It Together

If the grooming and the general cleanliness of your appearance give a positive impression, you can carry off any outfit. Make sure that shoes are well heeled, and clothes are clean, ironed, and free of stains. Fix any unraveling hems, loose threads, or missing buttons.

When your feet are uncomfortable, your mind is uncomfortable. Wear comfortable shoes that fit you and suit you. You won't be able to concentrate on anything else and remember your fabulous answers if your mind is preoccupied with pinching uncomfortable shoes. By the way, shoes should not need to be "broken in." Just buy a pair that fit you on day one.

If you are going to a special event, whether an interview or a special family occasion, I always advise that you should imagine yourself walking across an empty dance floor with people at each side and ask yourself the following questions about your outfit:

- Are you pulling at your hem?
- Are your fabrics uncomfortable, itchy, and scratchy?
- Are you pulling at your collar because it may be too tight?
- Are you pulling up a gaping neckline?
- Are you hoping that stressed buttons on that too-tight shirt are still in place?

Yet again, if your mind is on certain aspects of your outfit, your focus will be compromised.

Summary

In this chapter we learned about how workwear can help us:

- Make a good impression
- Be successful at an interview
- Give us an air of confidence
- Achieve our goals

Next Steps?

Take the Fun Interview Quiz in chapter 9.

Chapter 9:

Fun Interview Quiz

Interview Quiz

1. Qualifications are all you need to ensure that you get the job.

a. True

b. False

2. The outfit you should wear to an interview should be:

a. A formal outfit

b. An outfit you feel comfortable in

3. Should you bring a spare copy of your resumé/CV to the interview?

a. Yes

b. No

4. It is best to research the dress code of the organization and dress accordingly for the interview.

a. True

b. False

5. When should you arrive for your interview?

a. On time

b. Early

6. At the end of the interview you should mention your desired salary.

a. True

b. False

7. While waiting in reception for the interview one should:

a. Sit quietly and keep busy on your smartphone

b. Smile at the receptionist and put away your smartphone

8. If you have a raincoat and umbrella you should:

a. Leave them in reception

b. Bring them into the interview with you

9. Soon after the interview one should:

a. Send a thank-you email or note

b. Go over the questions and answers from the interview in your head

10. In advance of the interview, one should prepare for:

a. Hours

b. Days

Answers to Interview Quiz

1.b, 2. A, 3. A, 4. A, 5. B, 6. B, 7. B, 8. A, 9. A, 10. b

Note – Appropriate interview behavior may differ for different cultures. Have a look at www.executiveplanet.com. This will ensure that you are prepared for interviews in different countries and cultures.

To pull off all the above, you need to have confidence in yourself. By *appearing* confident, you will develop more confidence and achieve rewarding results.

Next Steps?

The next chapter covers confidence. Not an arrogant type of confidence but the belief in yourself so that you can project an air of competence. It's your own general feeling of self-esteem.

Section C:

All About Your Next Steps to Success

This section circles back to you and how you can grow in confidence for any situation by looking the part and looking after yourself.

Don't be afraid of gaining confidence. It's not arrogance, but a belief in yourself. Confidence is not thinking you are better than others but being self-assured about your own skills and the knowledge that you already have.

Chapter 10:

Confidence—Not Arrogance!

You won't put any of the advice in this book into practice if you don't work on your confidence. I wasn't always confident and I dreaded reading aloud in class and speaking up at staff meetings. I had to work on myself to learn to communicate confidently in small groups and then to a large audience. As a result, I've built up this repertoire of tips to help anyone gain confidence.

"If you hear a voice inside you say, 'You cannot paint,' then by all means paint and that voice will be silenced."

Vincent Van Gogh

We have all heard of the phrase "fake it until you make it." This doesn't mean faking your credentials or qualifications. Instead, it is an aim to project confidence while keeping it credible and true to yourself. This makes you more likable to others and makes it easier to develop a rapport.

Confidence is being content and at ease with yourself. It is not the same as conceit, but a belief in your own ability. By *appearing* confident, we can achieve so much more. By exuding an air of confidence in yourself, others will believe it.

Confidence will enable you to introduce yourself to people, network, make small talk and make inspiring speeches and influential presentations. If you believe in yourself, others will believe in you too.

The Least You Need to Know

By now, you can see that I love creating acrostic word lists! Each point is important, but you aren't expected to memorize them. I've highlighted the keyword or phrase to help it stick in your memory. Let's break down CONFIDENCE:

C - Connect with people. Don't shy away from eye contact and a smile will automatically connect you with people.

O - Overcome emotions that can be triggered in certain situations such as the classic "fight or flight" situations. Learn how to deflect conflict when someone is trying to push your buttons. There is no room for this in a workplace setting.

N - Networking is invaluable. We can do more when connected with others. Learn the art of small talk (this is covered in Part Two: To Promotion and Beyond). I like to say that your sixth sense is listening, being curious, and being aware of others. These are a big part of networking.

F - Focus on what you want to achieve and don't be afraid to assert yourself or speak up. Ambition brings inner confidence.

I - Identify who you are. What is your personality? Confidence is about knowing your own strengths and challenges. The more you know about yourself, the more at ease you will be with yourself and others. Confidence is about looking inwards before you can look outwards.

D - Drive your goals. Aim to achieve them. Visualize yourself achieving your goals.

E - Enthusiasm and confidence go hand in hand. Enthusiasm is infectious and will spread to others.

N - Never underestimate the power of a good first impression. First impressions are turned into lasting impressions when your behavior remains consistent—both good and bad. Remember you are always on stage, being observed.

C - Challenge yourself. You cannot improve your confidence levels if you ignore what you need to do to change. Don't be afraid to lean into your discomfort.

E - Everything is Possible!

"We are what we repeatedly do. Excellence then, is not an act, but a habit."

Aristotle

I've said it many times, but practice does make perfect.

Confidence is not as concerned with your intelligence quotient (IQ), but your emotional quotient (EQ). Emotional intelligence enables you to socialize effectively. This is a different type of smart. The art of developing your soft skills like effective communication and self-awareness are all part of your EQ. Your IQ may be fixed but EQ can be developed and eventually becomes less of an act, but more of a daily habit.

"When dealing with people, remember that you are not dealing with creatures of logic, but creatures of emotion."

Dale Carnegie

People skills are the foundation of confidence. By knowing yourself better, you can interact with others more successfully. You can also improve how you react to other peoples' behavior toward you and your reaction to others. Here's an acrostic to encapsulate the key factors of people skills:

P - Personal awareness

E - Emotional Awareness

O - Optimism

P - Personality

L - Language – Effective communication

E - Ethics and Etiquette (Good old-fashioned manners!)

Types of Confidence

We all gain confidence as we learn new skills and knowledge. Trying new things can be scary, especially if you are a little out of your comfort zone. Developing more confidence is just part of your journey to success. In this segment, we are going to look at different kinds of confidence. You can then give yourself a rating of where you fall on the confidence scale. This is your personal "confidence number" that you can review from time to time. It is not meant to be a criticism or discouragement. It is just another tool to gauge your level of progress.

Inner Confidence

Have you heard the term "impostor syndrome"? It is the feeling that you aren't good enough or skilled enough for the task, despite your qualifications and knowledge. Even well-known movie stars and athletes feel this way sometimes. Impostor syndrome is a form of self-doubt that causes negative self-talk. Ignore this. You choose what you want to believe of yourself. Be enthusiastic about yourself and your situation. Optimists are confident people.

Action 1: On a scale of 1 to 10, rate your inner confidence.

Physical Confidence

Do you portray confidence or an air of shyness and insecurity? The easiest way to give yourself a boost of confidence is to stand tall, sit up straight, and walk with purpose. Don't slouch or shuffle your feet. It also doesn't hurt to look your best. Go back and review the positive body language tips for an interview.

When you look good, you feel good. If I'm dressed appropriately for any occasion, whether it be an interview, a meeting, or a presentation I can hide my nerves more easily and give off an air of confidence. I call it my suit of armor.

Action 2: On a scale of 1 to 10, rate your physical confidence.

Social Confidence

Social confidence allows you to enjoy the presence of others. Being at ease in company makes people more comfortable and fosters a connection. Build relationships but be authentic. If you are prone to a bit of awkwardness, as we all are, it's best to laugh it off and "own" it. By not being overly dramatic or embarrassed if you spill coffee or get tongue-tied, you will actually come across as being more confident. Be true to yourself.

Now more than ever, having good social awareness and people skills is important due to technology distancing us from others as we text more than we speak to people. Also, due to the Covid pandemic, businesses have encouraged remote working fostering a certain amount of isolation. One person's idea of direct communication on a text message may come across as curt, bossy, or even angry. Learn to not react emotionally to other peoples' styles of communication. It is so easy to misinterpret someone's meaning or intention in a text message, email, or during a virtual meeting. Emotional awareness makes us more socially confident, better communicators, and helps us make better choices.

Action 3: On a scale of 1 to 10, rate your social confidence.

Summary

In this chapter we learned more about your confidence levels and how they can impact your actions and vice versa. Remember, rating your current level of confidence is just a tool to help you look for areas of improvement.

- People Skills
- Inner Confidence
- Physical Confidence
- Social Confidence

Next Steps?

Congratulations! You have made so many actions on your journey through the *Career Elevator*. Let's put it all to bed!

However, you won't be able to remember what you have learned or to put it into action if you don't get enough sleep. Yes, sleep!

Chapter 11:

Sleep Benefits for Your Life Goals and Dreams

"Sleep is an investment in the energy you need to be effective tomorrow."

Tim Roth

With the popularization of pedometers and advanced monitors, we can all find out how many steps we took or track our resting heart rate. These devices capture all aspects of our wellbeing, including the amount of sleep we get and the quality of sleep. Isn't it obvious how important sleep is when we see that sleep monitoring is a key feature of these devices? This confirms that our rest time is just as important for us as our active time! It may be a cliché, but rest is best.

Sleep hygiene is a serious part of our health and sleep is just as important as water, exercise, and even food. Has sleep become a luxury we all yearn for or a guilty pleasure? Do you feel afraid to admit that you need more sleep? We are sometimes afraid to admit to wanting and needing more sleep if it means leaving a work event early or turning down a request to work later. In many ways, making good sleeping habits a priority tends to be at odds with modern life.

Are we all thinking we are supposed to be busy, busy, busy, and not having enough time for sleep? It's OK to rest, recover, and reflect. Only you know how much sleep you need to recharge.

"Discover the great ideas that lie inside you by discovering the power of sleep."

Ariana Huffington

The Least You Need to Know

Tips for a good night's sleep:

- Reduce small screen time nearer bedtime.
- Read something. If you're reading this book, you obviously like books.
- Watch a comedy on television rather than something darker and more sinister right before bedtime.
- Don't overeat near bedtime or eat foods that may irritate your digestion. Stay away from caffeinated products and drinks late in the day.
- Appropriate exercise during the day can aid sleep.
- Try not to "work" where you sleep (I acknowledge that this is difficult for students)*.
- Make your bed every day and plump up your pillows if possible (This takes less than sixty seconds).
- Develop a routine both for going to sleep and waking for most days of the week.
- Have at least one glass of water by your bed.

*Students, if studying in your room, keep the bed area clear and free of clutter. Keep the books, your laptop, and folders in one area designated to work. Look at your space and consider how you could rearrange and declutter to achieve the balance between the two work and rest areas. Read the tips for a good night's sleep. Yes, they apply to you too!

Benefits of a Good Night's Sleep

- Better physical health
- Sleep is like an invisible vitamin
- A way to release the day's issues, anxieties, and problems
- Repairs and heals the bones, organs, muscles, and the mind
- Increased productivity
- Increased creativity
- Less tiredness, encouraging better judgment and concentration
- Better memory of prepared actions for the following day after sleep and rest

Sleep and Dream for Success

Don't be afraid to dream and wonder like a child—to question things. Many famous inventions have been the result of dreams. After all, most innovation and creativity involves solving problems, and during sleep our mind often processes problems. While we solve plenty of problems during waking hours, don't be afraid to learn from your own thoughts during sleep.

Keep a notebook by your bed and write down any thoughts on waking. Did you gain any insights about a certain solution or work out a conversation during a dream?

Go back to the Goal Setting chapter. What's on your mind? Don't dwell on a specific question. Instead, trust in your own mind to log in to what is needed. Automation and artificial intelligence cannot replace the power and productivity of the human mind. If your mind is active and proactive during the day, it will examine your goals and dreams passively while you rest.

Dream big, the bigger the better. Keep these dreams private unless you have very positive people to share them with. They are your own personal goals and there is no such thing as failure. Even dreaming is ambitious growth. Don't forget to dream while you're awake also!

Be around positive people. Make friends and surround yourself with people who want the best for you. Family are usually those people but not always a given or guaranteed.

Finally, to share more words of wisdom from our own W.B. Yeats in the poem below. Don't share your dreams unless people "tread softly" on them. Surround yourself with positive and supportive people as much as possible. That includes yourself!

"Aedh Wishes for the Cloths of Heaven"

Had I the heaven's embroidered cloths
Enwrought with golden and silver light,
The blue and the dim and the dark cloths
Of night and light and the half-light;
I would spread the cloths under your feet:
But I, being poor, have only my dreams;
I have spread my dreams under your feet;
Tread softly because you tread on my dreams.

W. B. Yeats

Conclusion to Part One: You're Hired

If you get the job, you've got it, but have you *made* it?

We've come to the end of the "You're Hired" section of the *Career Elevator*. If you stop reading here, you will have learned a lot. I hope the book has challenged you and has helped you come out of your comfort zone. If you stop here, then it's enough for you.

It's OK to stop here. You know what stage you're at. Remember that you can dip into sections of the book that apply to your specific situation. You may already know how to dress for success but need help starting a conversation.

If you're happy to leap further, you've successfully hopped through "You're Hired" and are ready to skip and even jump.

Going further through "To Promotion and Beyond" and even "I'm an Entrepreneur, Now What?" requires a commitment to excellence in everything you do, even when no one is looking. That's excellence and ethics. It means striving for excellence, not perfection, but aiming to be perfect in everything you do in your interpersonal interactions and the way you dress, smile, walk, talk, and your general ethics, etiquette, and manners.

Go the Extra Mile.

The first mile means that you make every possible effort to make a good impression, both visibly and audibly, to get a job. The extra mile means that you go beyond being good enough. You go from being good to great. You commit to managing every behavior, promise, and action, working harder, practicing new skills, and giving more.

You may have a job. But how do you climb the ladder, get noticed, get remembered, and get promoted?

If you want to stay in the same role and stay safe at work, keep your head down and get on with the job. If you want to be regarded as worth promoting, you need to work hard, but put your head up. You must aim to be visible, heard, and understood. This requires commitment, perseverance, and new skills.

Time to Play!

I love board games and find them to be a great way to demonstrate concepts and a fun way to remember terms and strategies. I developed business games as a result of my own passion for learning and teaching by doing and playing. The games were inspired by the letters in MBA. It's known as a "master of business administration" degree, but we give it another definition:

M Making

B Business

A an Adventure

Don't forget to access the free download of the board game *You're Hired*. This board game is easy to download and assemble. It's ideal for playing at home or in any group setting.

I was honestly delighted and heartened to see that Tim Draper who wrote the Foreword to this book and entrepreneur Robert T. Kiyosaki also developed board games for business education many years ago. I never knew this and I hope it's a case of "great minds think alike!"

Tim Draper wrote a book I recommend called *How to be The Startup Hero*.

Robert T. Kiyosaki wrote *Rich Dad, Poor Dad*, which is also a great read on entrepreneurship and investing.

Let's continue to Make Business an Adventure. Read on as your adventure unfolds!

PART TWO: TO PROMOTION AND BEYOND

Featuring:

Section A: Communicating with Others

Section B: Etiquette and Manners

Section C: Communicating in Public

Section A:

Communicating with Others

Communication—whether it is with one person or a whole conference room—is the most important skill to make yourself visible to others at work. Speaking with people more senior to us can be daunting and challenging at first but I'll say it again, practice makes perfect. You will learn how to network, make small talk, and have meaningful conversations. That's how you make successful connections and lasting impressions.

So how do you communicate? Every day we communicate with others through talking, writing, and even making silent signals. Good communication skills trump many other capabilities, and they can give you an edge or advantage.

Technical skills and what you learned in "You're Hired" can get you in the door – but more soft skills will keep you in the job, get you noticed, and promoted. Learn how to make positive impressions and develop lasting successful connections.

You are aiming to connect, impress, and influence people who you work with and work for. In other words, people at all levels at your place of work. Connecting with people within and outside the organization will open many more connections and successful relationships.

Now that you have a job, you need to get noticed. That means being visible, listening to others, and speaking up when you have something to contribute to the discussion. Don't shy away from making presentations and delivering persuasive speeches. The three sections ahead will equip you to make more positive first impressions and lasting successful connections. The three sections ahead will lead you "To Promotion and Beyond."

Fasten your seatbelt!

Chapter 1:

Listening and the True Art of Conversation

"The word *listen* contains the same letters as the word *silent*."
Alfred Brendel

There is a common equation that says we need to "listen twice as much as we speak." This is great advice for all of us, whether it is in an office or at a party. Connections start with conversations and listening is a key skill in making conversation. Listening will help your networking skills.

This involves concentrating, questioning, taking note of what is being said, and physically appearing to be a good listener. As you listen more, you will notice that other people really like to talk! A true conversation connects you with people. No one will ever feel you are taking something seriously if you appear unwilling to listen. Be present. Shut your mind down to nothing else but the current conversation.

"Most people do not listen with the intent to understand; they listen with the intent to reply."
Stephen R. Covey

Read that quote again. Stephen Covey wrote the worldwide bestseller, *The 7 Habits of Highly Effective People*. In it, he outlined some of the best habits that will help you in all aspects of your life, including business relationships. One of these habits is active listening, which is not thinking about what you want to say next when the other person is speaking. Active listening involves concentrating and being in the present. Work at it and it will soon become a good habit. Good conversations involve both listening and questioning. Taking turns to speak and listen is the true art of conversation. Want to listen.

The Least You Need to Know

- Look and behave like a good listener
- React (use body language to show that you have heard what the other person has said)
- Stop talking (do not interrupt)
- Use empathy
- Check (clarify by asking questions and paraphrasing what was said by that person)
- Remain unemotional (too much thinking ahead can distract you)
- Concentrate (allow nothing to distract you)
- Look at the other person
- Note key points (edit what you hear to retain key points)

Learn to take notes in your head if it's not an appropriate occasion to take notes in writing.

The Art of Listening

Listening really is an art and many people can be horrible listeners. How many times have you tried to get a word in edgeways? while someone else just keeps talking? Have you ever poured your heart out to someone only to have them launch into their own sob story? True active listening requires you to be present and engaged.

You need to open your mind to the person and the situation. It may be tempting to get ahead of what they are saying and assume you know the problem or what they will say next. Just listen carefully to get a fuller picture of what they are saying without jumping in. Be patient and first try to understand what they are saying or asking.

If this is a friend, you may initially ask if they just need someone to listen or if they are looking for solutions. It is good to know if they just need to vent and blow off steam. Oftentimes, people just need to be "heard" and aren't asking for your opinion or solutions.

Back in a work situation, there are ways that you can make yourself heard and ensure that you do the same for others. Here are a few tips:

- Reconfirm and occasionally paraphrase what the person has said. This shows that you are actively listening and understanding what is being said.
- Wait your turn to speak. Be patient. Knowing when *not* to talk is as important as knowing when to talk.
- Don't dominate the conversation. Active listening means just that.
- Respond with positive body language and gestures (eye contact, leaning in, smiling, nodding, not fidgeting, etc.).
- Take in what the person is saying and remember to put their name in your mind and repeat it to yourself.

"One of the most sincere forms of respect is actually listening to what another has to say."

Bryant H. McGill

When people feel that they have your undivided attention, it makes them feel good. When you say someone's name, it makes them feel good. When you recall and remember something that that person told you previously, it makes them feel good. These steps all contribute to others associating that good feeling with you.

Remembering Names

Remembering someone's name is crucial in the workplace and forgetting a name can be one of those things that gives us anxiety. Haven't you heard someone say, "I'm horrible with names," at work or at a party? It happens to us all at some point.

To help you remember someone's name, register the name of the person in your head and use it occasionally during the conversation. We all love being called by our own name. It's easier to connect and have a positive conversation when we call the other person by their name occasionally. It is also easier to remember their name once you have said it a few times.

Remember the names of everyone at work at all levels of the organization. Use names as a win-win way to start conversations and make connections. Some of the most successful leaders can walk through a building or a factory and know everyone by name. It's a very useful skill to learn. If your own name is unusual or hard to pronounce, come up with an easy reminder you can tell the person. You are letting them know the correct way to say your name while helping them avoid awkward mispronunciations.

Tips for Remembering Names

Commitment – Want to remember the person's name. Make it a priority.

Concentration – Deliberately register the name in your head.

Association – Sometimes it's easier to associate the name with someone else you know with that name. It might even be the first letter of their name which triggers the memory of the name. It might even be a place or object you can associate the person's name to.

Repetition – Repeat the person's name during the conversation.

"Most of the successful people I've known are the ones who do more listening than talking."

Bernard Baruch

Listening well will help your networking skills with your supervisors or managers. This involves concentrating, questioning, taking note of what is being said, and appearing to be a good listener. A true conversation connects you with people. No one will ever feel you are taking something seriously if you appear unwilling to listen.

Summary

In this chapter we learned about listening and how important it is during conversations.

- Listening twice as much as we speak
- Responding with positive body language
- Remembering people's names

Next Steps

We mentioned the importance of responding to others with positive body language and gestures. But can you read other people's body language?

Read on to learn how to interpret the silent signals that people give during a conversation. There's more to listening and interacting with people than just words.

Chapter 2:

Managing and Reading Body Language

"The most important thing in communication is hearing what isn't said."

Peter Drucker

What Do We Say When We're Not Speaking?

Nonverbal behavior is indeed a language. We are always observing other people's body language, even in interactions on TV and media. We unconsciously make judgments based on the body language of others. And others judge us, making judgments on how they think and feel about us or about what we are saying or doing.

Your body language is part of a conversation. You need to be aware of your own body language and also need to be able to read the other person's body language. If you have ever watched a televised court trial or procedure, you will see how the person's body language or expressions make you trust or disbelieve them.

Your body language can leave a lingering message even after you have left the room. Posture, walking, sitting, standing, mannerisms, gestures, and facial expressions are all aspects of our body language. These, as well as our handshake, send strong messages—good or bad.

Consider what words you would like people to use to describe you. What words would you like people to attribute to your behavior? Words associated with confidence or words that convey a lack of effort or care? This is all part of your personal brand. You need a consistent, positive, and powerful personal and professional brand to be successful and influential.

Actions Speak Louder than Words

Make sure that you match your behavior—and your body language—to your spoken words. This will increase your self-esteem and confidence. We are also influenced by our own body language and if we feel that we are projecting a positive message through our actions, we gain confidence. Facial expressions are the most telling aspects of body language.

When we have a rapport with people, we unconsciously find ourselves mirroring their own body language. If you consciously want to build a rapport with somebody, mirroring their actions and gestures when speaking to them is an effective way to achieve this.

"The eyes are the window to your soul."

William Shakespeare

The Least You Need to Know

Eye Contact

Maintain eye contact during all conversations and beware of your blinking rate. The slower your blinking rate, the more confident you appear.

Facial Expression

A smile is very powerful so the best way to begin a conversation for a positive outcome is to smile. Do not grin from ear to ear, just smile.

Maintaining a gentle smile will keep you from making any negative expressions such as frowning or smirking. Keep your hands away from your face. Nodding, smiling, and tilting the head slightly show that we are interested in what the other person is saying.

Posture

Good posture is a strong message to send while standing and walking. Good posture enhances confidence. Stand tall and sit up straight to appear focused and project confidence.

Movement

Walk with confidence and purpose. When walking, aim your feet straight ahead of you and take long steps. Aim to be midway between striding very slowly and rushing. Avoid marching, scampering, or shuffling your feet.

Stand Up Straight and Tall

- Lift your ribcage up and out slightly
- Roll your shoulders back
- Stand with feet side-by-side
- Keep your weight equally on both feet
- Do not lean on anything as it reduces your level of authority
- Breathe slowly and evenly
- Lift your chin slightly
- Imagine puppet strings are holding up your head

Sit Up Straight

- Keep legs closed with both feet on the floor
- Don't slouch or sprawl on your chair
- Sit with your back firmly to the back of the chair
- Rest palms loosely on your lap
- Keep still and avoid fidgeting
- If sitting at a desk at a meeting, avoid shuffling papers or fidgeting with pens

The more aware you become of your own body language and its impact on the messages you send out, the more confident you will become. You will also become more successful at reading the body language of others. This is a two-way conversation, and you will have an advantage if you are able to read body language.

We all make gestures, so make sure yours are positive. Avoid distracting gestures. When pointing, make sure that the palm of your hand is either sideways or upward. Otherwise, your pointing gesture can look too strong and forceful.

The following actions are negative, ranging from disinterest to impatience and even dishonesty:

- Crossing and uncrossing legs
- Foot and finger tapping
- Folding and unfolding arms
- Resting the head in a hand
- Shoulder shrugging
- Fiddling with nails, pens, notebooks, etc.
- Looking away while you're speaking
- Flicking or touching hair constantly
- Rubbing the face or the hands together
- Hiding part of the face with the hand
- Excessive eye movement
- Constant rubbing or touching your nose
- Touching the face more than usual

Action Idea: Use your smartphone to record yourself reading a page or two of a book. You will soon notice any body language issues that need to be addressed. Remember, these are only habits that can be fixed.

Summary

In this chapter, we learned about the impact of our own body language and tips for reading others' body language.

- Facial Expressions
- Eye Contact
- Posture
- Movement

Next Steps?

Now, that we have covered effective communication with others through listening and positive body language, you're now ready to introduce yourself to new people and use that personal elevator pitch you have perfected.

Meeting with potential employers or future colleagues requires networking and small talk skills.

Chapter 3:

Networking and the Art of Small Talk

"Networking is more about 'farming' than it is about 'hunting.' It's about cultivating relationships."

Dr. Ivan Misner, the founder and chairman of the Business Networking Organization (BNI)

Successful networking ensures that you make connections, develop new contacts, and meet new people. To do so, you have to introduce yourself. Get out of your comfort zone and start conversations with new people. As always, practice makes perfect.

Remember your personal elevator pitch when someone asks you, "Tell me about yourself."

Go back and revisit Chapter 2 from "You're Hired." Use your hand to remember the five points about you that you want to share. Your elevator pitch will change as you progress through life but essentially it introduces you, your current situation, and your future goals. It should be no more than thirty seconds long.

Now you have the confidence to answer the question "tell me about yourself." Delivering your personal elevator pitch is a great way to start a conversation.

Networking is vital, whether you find yourself at impromptu meetings or formal networking events such as conferences.

The Least You Need to Know

- Stand up straight
- Smile and remember eye contact
- Greet the person
- Say "hello, it's nice to meet you," repeating the person's name
- Use people's titles such as Mr., Ms., Dr., etc., until they ask you to call them by their first name
- Name badges should be worn on the right shoulder. This makes is easier to read a person's name
- Use a firm handshake always
- Don't invade people's personal space
- Be present
- Ask questions
- Listen to the answers
- Follow up with people after meeting them

How to Become an Expert at Small Talk

The Art of Questioning

Questions are a good way to start a conversation, but it is most important to listen to the answers. It works both ways. Most people love to be asked questions and talk about themselves. Some more than others, as I'm sure you've experienced when someone tells you their entire life story when you only asked, "How are you?"

At the beginning of a conversation, you can use closed questions that require short simple answers. Make sure to listen to the person's answers. This enables you to ask more open questions linked to their previous answers. This is where you find out more about the person and their interests. The greatest interviewers on television use this technique. It helps develop a natural conversation with a guest. In your life, building upon your questions based on someone's responses helps you build a rapport with others.

This is a two-way street, so reciprocate and reveal something of yourself so that people can relate to you. However, do be aware that in the age of social media, oversharing is a new phenomenon. Maintain a balance between revealing something about yourself and oversharing. You both like dogs? That's great. You just spent ten minutes talking about your big, dramatic break-up? Probably not the best topic.

Become familiar with various current topics in news, media, sport, entertainment, and the arts. It's natural to like people who are like you, but networking requires you to make small talk with a variety of people. Be present and listen. Even if you don't like sports, you can just say "that sounds like it was a good game."

If someone offers you their business card, look at it carefully and read it. Keep it in your hand for the time you are in conversation and when you put it away, put it respectfully and carefully in your jacket pocket or a clean pocket of your bag. Even if you don't plan on needing their services, treat the card—and the person—with respect. Only offer your own business card if the other person asks you for more information about you or your company. Hand it slowly to the person so that they can see and read the information.

Handshake Tips

How firm is your handshake? Practice developing a firm, confident handshake. Try to get the balance right between the strong "bone crusher" and the damp, weak "limp fish." Touch is another of the senses used when making a first impression and people remember good and bad handshakes.

Look the other person in the eye and smile. Extend your hand in front of you, parallel to the floor. Close your hand over the other hand when your thumbs meet. Shake your hand from your elbow, not from the wrist as this makes your hand almost "jiggle." Shake the other person's hand firmly two to three times.

Do not invade someone's personal space. Try imagining that you have a hula hoop around you, keeping one to two arm lengths away from the other person. That is the ideal distance to remain from somebody when shaking their hand.

Some people think that women need a light and dainty handshake and may just grab your fingers. That can be condescending for the receiver and may be interpreted as if you don't see that person as an equal. It is a safe bet to just shake everyone's hand in a firm handshake every time.

Top Tip - Carry your laptop, bag, notebook, or papers in your left hand. This leaves your right hand free by your side and ready to shake hands when meeting someone.

Introductions

Introducing people to others is very important but can be very confusing. You show respect by introducing the most senior or important person to the other person. To do this, you set it up by saying the name of the least important person first.

It is complicated, but remember who is the most important person. For example, you could say, “John, this is Ann Hughes, our director.” Or you could say, “John, I would like to introduce Ann, our director.” So, it is like you are building up to the name of the more important person. Almost as if they make a grand entrance to the introduction.

Small Talk Checklist

- Ask people their opinions
- Keep it personal – tell a story about yourself
- Stay away from controversial topics
- Listen more than you speak
- Ask good questions, then be quiet and listen
- Don’t dominate the conversation
- Repeat and remember people’s names
- Be mindful of different cultures - www.executiveplanet.com

Summary

In this chapter, we learned about networking and making small talk.

- Introducing yourself
- Where to wear a name badge
- A powerful handshake
- The art of questioning
- The art of small talk

Next Steps?

Knowing polite and appropriate actions and behaviors for any occasion can give you greater confidence and help you make a lasting good impression. Etiquette is politeness and good old-fashioned manners. Ethics are a combination of your manners, values, and principles. They are what you do when no one is looking.

Section B:

Etiquette and Manners

When you know how to behave in any situation, you will be more comfortable and relaxed and able to speak confidently to others. Your mind will not be flustered trying to think of the silent rules of how to behave in certain situations. There are ways to interact with others both personally and professionally that make lasting impressions. There are ways to behave at dinner and lunch that can either make or break us. Read on to learn the basics of etiquette and just how important etiquette and manners are.

Chapter 4:

Etiquette

"Teach love, generosity, good manners and some of that will drift from the classroom to the home and who knows, the children will be educating the parents."

Roger Moore

Manners will open any door!

Manners are guidelines to help us as we interact with the people around us, employing appropriate actions, appearance, and words that will help us build successful relationships.

Your job skills will get you in the door, but your people skills are what will ensure that you always make a good impression and even earn you a promotion. Etiquette and manners never draw attention to themselves, they are never distracting. You want people to focus on you and what you are discussing, not be distracted by you reaching across the dinner table or chewing with your mouth open.

It simply involves being considerate to others and being aware of how any actions or situations can affect others. Our behavior affects everyone we meet, and etiquette helps us build positive relationships. Did you ever get a positive feeling when someone didn't hold the door open when your hands were full? Probably not. Knowing more about etiquette gives you the confidence to handle any situation with ease, enabling you to relax and be yourself.

"Please" and "thank you" are words that are not said enough. Just because some workplaces are less formal than others, doesn't mean that people have stopped caring about manners. No matter how informal or formal, good social skills are still essential to your professional and personal success. Sincerity and good manners can charm and have a positive influence on others.

Etiquette = Manners + Principles

There was a song in the '80s by Fun Boy Three and Bananarama called "It Ain't What You Do It's the Way That You Do It." They go on to sing, "It ain't what you say...." In other words, you can get a positive reaction to any request if you remember this:

It's not what you ask for, it's the way that you ask.

Good old-fashioned manners and proper behavior in social settings are all about common sense. It is essentially back to basics. Being considerate and having empathy for others and treating people the way you would want to be treated. Don't get down when other people don't have good manners. Just be a positive example and do the kind things anyway.

The Least You Need to Know

The six principles of etiquette and being well mannered when interacting with others:

1. Honesty
2. Sincerity
3. Truthfulness
4. Cooperation
5. Respect
6. Consideration

Remember the manners of introductions and business card etiquette. Good manners and etiquette further enhance your networking skills. It is the combination of the ability to introduce yourself and others, having a good handshake, and the correct body language for work situations.

Respect and consideration will ensure that you behave well with people at all levels in an organization and leave lasting positive impressions. Be happy for the successes of people around you, whether they be friends, family, or colleagues. They didn't earn these successes without hard work. Envy and jealousy of other peoples' success are bad manners. This type of negative behavior will only limit your own personal success.

Good manners are also an awareness of how your own actions might possibly affect others. This applies to personal habits also such as putting your hand over your mouth when yawning to leaving the room to blow your nose with a tissue. Knowing how to behave well with others will give you the confidence to meet more people, speak more to them, and make more positive lasting impressions. Knowledge of manners and etiquette will make you more comfortable and less worried about how to behave around people more senior than you. This will ensure that you are at ease so that you can concentrate on being yourself and engage in meaningful conversations.

Your job skills will get you in the door, but your people skills are what will land you a promotion. Etiquette and manners are essential to your people skills. Bad manners don't whisper, they scream and draw attention in a negative way. Good etiquette and manners never distract negatively so that people can focus on you and what you are saying. Like a smile, good manners are contagious and if you show respect, you will in turn be shown respect.

Etiquette at Work

- Help or assist anyone in need such as holding a door, helping put on a coat, or helping to carry something.
- Say please when asking for something.
- Say thank you for small things like someone holding the door for you.
- Ask your colleagues how they are and show an interest in them and their families.
- Ensure that any new people or visitors are welcomed warmly and shown where everything is in the building.
- If you have something private to say to someone, don't whisper into their ear in front of other people. Speak privately away from others.
- Use people's titles such as Mr., Ms., Dr., etc., until they ask you to call them by their first name.
- Introduce yourself first when you don't know everyone.
- Allow others to go first and before you such as making a coffee, at the water cooler, getting into an elevator, approaching a buffet, or taking seats at a table.
- Turn your smartphone off before you go into a meeting. Digital etiquette is covered in the next chapter. We can become very self-absorbed when we overuse our smartphones which makes us less aware of those around us.

Ethics

What do you do when no one is looking?

Ethics are all about your values and integrity. Ethics are about you managing your own thoughts and actions to become a person who values equality, truth, honesty, and cooperation. We make decisions based on our personal ethics every day. Did you find a wallet in a store and turn it in to lost and found? Do you sneak into work late and have someone cover for you? Are you texting on your phone whenever the boss leaves the office? These are just a few examples of how our ethics dictate our behavior.

Summary

In this chapter, we learned about the power and positive effect of Etiquette

- Ethics
- Honesty
- Respect
- Consideration of others

Next Steps?

We are all consumed by technology as it plays such an important role in all aspects of our lives. Digital Etiquette ensures that we manage our smart tools instead of them managing us.

Read on!

Chapter 5:

Digital Etiquette

"Technology should improve your life... not become your life."
Billy Cox

Living in a digital world requires us to practice digital etiquette. What kind of manners do you show online? Do you feel less connected to people in a virtual setting? Technology is a wonderful tool for collaboration, communication, and creation. Technology provides us with an efficient platform for marketing ourselves or a business to a global audience.

It's true that technology has enhanced and advanced our communication and connection competencies in a particular way, but this type of virtual connection can also foster a lack of real connection. As human beings, we are wired to connect with ourselves and with others. Technology has reduced the need to speak to other people or even meet with others face-to-face. People skills are now more important than ever.

One area of digital etiquette that we need to address is smartphone etiquette. With the advent of smartphones, it has become increasingly hard to be present when you're interacting with people. Smartphones interrupt the flow of meaningful conversations by distracting us. To have a meaningful conversation, turn it off so that you can remain completely focused on the other person and the conversation.

The Least You Need to Know

Smartphone Etiquette:

1. Don't let your smartphone ring if the ringtone will disturb others around you.
2. If taking a call is necessary, speak quietly and keep it brief and to the point.
3. When speaking on a smartphone, you need to be especially careful not to shout.
4. Never say anything confidential, personal, or private if others can overhear you.
5. Listen to your voice message. Does it give the impression you wish for?
6. Consider the volume, pace, and pitch of your voice. This must match and reflect you and your spoken message.
7. Constant recording of events can make us miss out on the actual enjoyable experience of a concert or a once-in-a-lifetime event. Be present and live in the moment. You'll enjoy it much more!
8. Develop resilience to influential media messages, be equipped to examine news feeds on phones and other digital devices to be able to interpret which news is real and which is not. Use discernment in filtering out scams or misleading websites.
9. Oversharing is a new phenomenon with the rise of obsession with social media.
10. The less you share on social media, the more confident you should feel professionally.

Email Etiquette

- Answer emails within forty-eight hours.
- Do not use all capital letters—it can be interpreted as shouting.
- Keep it brief and use simple but clear language.
- Use the BCC (blind copy) function if emailing a large group that do not know each other. Never finish a phone call or an email in a negative tone.

If you take a telephone message for another person, make sure to write down the name of the person and their number. Repeat it back to them to ensure that you have the correct details. Don't be like Hugh Grant's flatmate in *Notting Hill* that forgot to tell him that Julia Roberts had called and then neglected to write down the name or remember the pseudonym she was using. It is a funny scene in the movie, but probably won't be too funny if it happens to you at work.

Etiquette Fun Quiz

1. At a business meeting, you should:

a. Introduce yourself and others to people

b. Just casually join in the conversation

2. At a business event, you should wear your name badge on your:

a. Left shoulder

b. Right shoulder

3. When thanking someone for a personal gift, you should:

a. Send an email or text

b. Send a handwritten card or note

4. If you meet a person again at an event but cannot remember their name, do you:

a. Smile, say nothing, and hope that somebody comes along who may know their name

b. Apologize, admitting that you cannot remember their name

5. At a business event do you do the following with your business card:

a. Wait to be asked for your business card

b. Offer your business card to everyone you meet

6. When a person gives you their business card, do you:

a. Take it and put it in your back pocket

b. Look at the card, read the text, and make sure to be visibly putting it in a place of respect

7. When taking a telephone message, should you:

a. Take the name and number

b. Ask the person to spell their name and read their number back to them

8. If introduced to somebody while you are seated, do you:

a. Stand up and shake their hand

b. Smile and say hello

9. If you must take an important call while in company, do you:

a. Speak quietly during the conversation

b. Move away and take the call out of earshot of people and finish it as soon as possible

10. If you forget to turn off your phone in company and you receive a call from a friend, do you:

a. Answer and briefly tell the person that you will call them back

b. Text the person where you are, who you are with, and that you will call them back later.

11. If you are introduced to speak to somebody for the first time but you don't know anything about them, do you:

a. Ask them friendly questions about themselves

b. Tell them all about yourself

12. When in a conversation, you show the person that you are interested by:

a. Leaning in very closely to listen

b. Use positive actions by nodding, smiling, and maintaining eye contact

13. When introduced to somebody for the first time, do you:

a. Shake their hand with both hands, nodding enthusiastically while leaning in

b. Shake their hand with your right hand and leave enough personal space as if you both have a hula hoop around your waists.

14. When in a conversation with a group, do you:

a. Pay attention and maintain eye contact, remembering to blink

b. Smile while looking around the room for other people you must speak to

15. When in a conversation with people and an uncomfortable or contentious topic arises, do you:

a. Tell them about your opinion on the topic

b. Make a polite effort to change the subject

16. When visiting a big organization for a meeting, make sure to be polite and friendly to:

a. Every employee you meet

b. The most important person that you are meeting

Answers to Etiquette Quiz

1.a, 2. b, 3. b, 4. b, 5. a, 6. b, 7. b, 8. a, 9. b, 10. a, 11. a, 12. b, 13. b, 14. a, 15. b, 16. a

Summary

In this chapter, we learned about managing our digital etiquette:

- Smartphone Etiquette
- Telephone Message Checklist
- Email Etiquette

Next Steps?

Worried about which utensil is the salad fork? Dining etiquette requires us to have respect and consideration for the table, the waiting staff, the dinner host, and other diners.

You never know when you might need to impress at a working lunch or dinner.

Can you juggle your cutlery?

Chapter 6:

Juggling Cutlery

"The way you treat your food on your plate is a reflection of the way you treat people in your life. Learning how to dine teaches you not just how to eat but how to treat people."

Rajiv Talreja

Whether you want to impress at a working lunch, a dinner party, or a family occasion, you can have fun with friends, family, and colleagues practicing good table manners. Don't underestimate the power of good table manners for making a great first impression.

Due to busy lifestyles and the obsession with technology, conversational mealtime has almost become a thing of the past. That is where people originally learned their table manners, literally around the family table.

Remember the movie *Pretty Woman* where Julia Roberts's character agonized over knowledge of place setting and correct cutlery for each course in a fancy French restaurant? She wanted to make a good impression. Instead, she wrestled with a pair of tongs and ended up launching an escargot (snail) across the room. We probably have similar stories of dining table mishaps that felt embarrassing.

If you Google examples of formal and informal table place settings, you will see that they differ from simple to complex. When interacting with people from different countries and cultures for the first time over a meal it would be advisable to consult an excellent website: www.executiveplanet.com.

Practice laying a table correctly. After all, we learn more by doing. The etiquette of dining and table manners centers around the following three principles.

1. Respect for the table

2. Respect for the host

3. Consideration of other diners

Of course, as practiced by Julia Roberts in *Pretty Woman*, if in doubt, wait for others to commence eating before reaching for the cutlery yourself!

Once you have read this chapter you will find it difficult to avoid watching out for people with good table manners (or bad) at future meals!

"Don't let your hunger for success neglect your table manners."
#GriffWisdom

Table Manners

The Least You Need to Know

- If there are named place cards on a table, sit where you are allocated whether you like it or not.
- Place your napkin on your lap once seated.
- Your side plate is on your left.
- Your drinking glass is above your knife to the right.
- Keep personal items such as keys, sunglasses, and smartphones off the table.
- Hold cutlery correctly with index fingers pointing forward.
- Rest cutlery on your plate during the meal, never on the table.
- If someone asks you to pass the salt, pass both salt and pepper. They always stay together.
- Break off or tear your bread roll, and butter one piece at a time.
- If you need to use butter, mustard, jam, or any other condiments, place some on your plate and then use it as you need it. They never go straight to your food.
- Never push your plate away from you when finished your meal.
- If a sandwich or burger is bigger than your hand, cut it in half before eating.

Like it or not, table manners are the most important measure of etiquette. Good table manners can be researched, learned, acquired, and practiced. With practice, good table manners can in fact become a good habit that will help you for a lifetime.

Below are extreme examples of dining etiquette. The principles of all table manners below are associated with the view that the table is regarded as a sacred or special place, prepared by the restaurant or host, and demands respect from the start to the finish of the meal.

Let's take it from the top!

Approaching the Table

Many social events involve busy tables set for ten people, so the general rule is for people to enter their seats from the left. Pulling out a chair for *anyone* is very polite and very acceptable. Don't get hung up on gender issues here. I've often held out a chair for a man at a busy table if I got there first.

At the Table

Adhere to the name place allocation if there are name places. Sit where you are allocated whether you like it or not. Refrain from placing personal items on the table such as smart phones, sunglasses, car keys, handbags, purses, hats, and scarves.

Place your napkin on your lap once seated; this shows good manners. Your napkin will either be folded straight in front of you or to your left under your cutlery or on your side plate. Location may differ, but it will be neatly folded and waiting for you to use it.

Before Eating

Cutlery is always arranged in alphabetical order from your left to your right: fork, knife, spoon. Your side plate is on your left. Your glass is above your knife to the right. If in doubt regarding the correct use of cutlery, work from the outside in and or wait for the host to choose which cutlery to use first.

It is impossible to show examples of every option for place settings as they do change according to the venue, meal, and occasion. Just remember that your drinking glasses are on your right and your side/bread plate is on your left.

Absolute Rule: Wait until everybody at the table is served before beginning to eat. The host is the only person who can overrule this by telling people to eat immediately to prevent dishes from getting cold.

Cutlery

Cutlery sits on a napkin or on a tablecloth (if there is one) before a meal. Once you start eating, the cutlery rests on the plate and never on the table.

Hold cutlery correctly with index fingers pointing forward (avoid holding cutlery in a clenched hand like a dagger!). Always keep your elbows down while eating. Never ever put a knife in your mouth.

We officially *eat* soup, we don't drink it! Scoop soup away from you to avoid spills when raising the soup spoon to your mouth. You may tilt the bowl away from yourself to finish eating your soup. Remember to take the soup spoon out of the bowl when finished and leave it resting on the underplate.

Place enough butter, jam, mustard, sauces, and such on your plate and use small amounts as you need them. Any communal dishes or sauces need to be placed on your own plate before you eat them. They don't go straight onto your food and you don't dip your bread into the mustard jar. Take the amount you think you'll need and use them one portion at a time. Break off or tear your bread roll and butter one piece at a time before eating that piece.

Passing Food

If asked to pass either the salt or pepper, pass both. Always ask for condiments to avoid reaching over people.

Don't pick up any food or cutlery you have dropped. Believe it or not, this is the job of the waiting staff. The reason for this? They can take it away and replace it with a new clean one. Should you pick it up yourself, you will end up placing dirty cutlery on the table which would show a lack of respect for the table.

Eating

Cut and eat one bite of your food at a time. This allows you to pause eating to make conversation at the table. Imagine your plate as a compass. Cutlery always rests on your plate NE and NW, never on the table or on the tablecloth. Sit up straight and never lean over food. Keep your mouth closed when chewing food.

Leaving the Table

If you must leave the table, leave your napkin on the chair. Once a meal has commenced, a napkin will no longer be spotless and therefore will stay on your lap. However, it should be placed on the chair if you need to leave the table. Only place your napkin on the table at the very end of the meal before standing to leave.

Finishing the Meal

Never push your plate away from you when finished your meal, leave it exactly where it was placed in front of you originally. Pretend your plate is a clock and place your knife and fork together at 3:50 as a signal to the waiting staff that you are finished eating. This signal may change for different cultures.

Buffet Meals and Finger Food

Buffet meals are a more casual dining situation. Be polite and allow people to get into the queue before you if you are speaking with them. Wait for others to join you at the table before eating.

Finger food is often served at a casual dining event where people are most likely standing together in groups. Food is passed throughout the room. There should be plates or napkins available to you.

It shows good manners to put the food you've taken on a plate or napkin first, before eating. Do not eat straight from the serving platter. If a sandwich or burger is bigger than your hand, cut it in half before eating.

Table Manners Quiz

1. While getting into your seat, should you approach the chair from the:

a. Right

b. Left

2. Food should be passed to the:

a. Right

b. Left

3. Are personal items permissible on the table?

a. Yes

b. No

4. Put your napkin on your lap:

a. Immediately

b. When your food is served

5. If leaving the table, leave your napkin:

a. On the table

b. On your chair

6. After the meal, leave your napkin:

a. On the table

b. On your chair

7. Before buttering your bread roll, do you:

a. Cut it

b. Tear a piece off

8. Eat finger foods:

a. Straight from the serving plate

b. After you have placed them on a plate or napkin

9. Eat communal food such as side vegetables:

a. Straight from the serving dish

b. After you have placed them on your plate

10. Start eating:

a. When you are served

b. When everyone at the table is served

11. When eating soup, scoop the spoon:

a. Toward you

b. Toward the back of the bowl

12. After eating soup, place the spoon:

a. In the bowl

b. Resting on the under plate

13. In between uses, place cutlery:

a. On the plate

b. On the tablecloth

14. If someone asks you to pass the salt only, do you:

a. Pass the salt

b. Pass both the salt and pepper

15. At the table, where do you keep your smartphone and other personal items?

a. On the table

b. Safely in your bag or pocket

16. Which piece of cutlery is never put in your mouth?

a. Knife

b. Fork

17. Cutlery is arranged from left in alphabetical order.Your fork is on your:

a. Left

b. Right

18. Your drinking glass is on your:

a. Left

b. Right

19. If a burger or sandwich is bigger than the palm of your hand, should you?

a. Pick it up in both hands and enjoy it

b. Cut it in half and eat one part at a time

20. To signal to the server that you are finished eating:

a. Place your cutlery together on the plate

b. Push your plate away from you

Answers to Table Manners Quiz

1.b, 2. a, 3. b, 4. a, 5. b, 6. a, 7. b, 8. b, 9. b, 10. b, 11. b, 12. b, 13. a, 14. b, 15. b, 16. a, 17. a, 18. b, 19. b, 20. a

Summary

In this chapter, we learned about the importance of table manners for making a good impression

- Respect for the table
- Respect for the host and other diners
- Sharing food
- Place settings
- Handling cutlery

Next Steps?

Now that we are more comfortable communicating and interacting with people by what we say and do, it may be time to get out of our comfort zone and speak up and speak out to larger groups. Public speaking involves speaking at meetings, making speeches, and presenting.

Section C:

Communicating in Public

By now, you should be very comfortable speaking in small groups at meetings or events. Your skills in listening, networking, and small talk will enable you to speak with others in a relaxed but professional way. Knowing basic etiquette will keep your mind worry-free so that you can join in on any conversation. When joining others at a meal, your basic table manners will allow you to enjoy speaking with others and making a good impression.

Public speaking, making presentations, and writing emails and speeches are ways in which we communicate with the wider public. Communicating in public is one of the most frightening challenges for many people. This section will help you get over the nerves and deliver successful and correctly written speeches and presentations with ease and confidence.

Chapter 7:

How to Master Nerves and the Art of Public Speaking

"There are only two types of speakers in the world: 1. The nervous and 2. The liars."

Mark Twain

When I was presenting to new audiences for the first time, I practiced for hours, recording my opening lines, and listening to them constantly until I was comfortable listening to myself say these lines aloud. Now, we have smartphones which can provide all the capability for these rehearsals to take place.

Once you have memorized and delivered your opening lines "off by heart," you will have control of yourself and continue, speaking positively with confidence and flow.

We can all learn, practice, rehearse, and produce a pitch publicly. It's all about you and your preparation. Once you're passionate and you feel that you are knowledgeable enough on the topic, it gets easier and your nerves settle more quickly.

This chapter deals with the general introduction of you acquiring your new skill as a public speaker and being comfortable with the sound of your own voice. Even speaking up at formal or informal meetings will become easier with a few tips from this chapter.

- First, be passionate, knowledgeable, and enthusiastic about your topic. We become more confident, sincere, and convincing when we believe in what we are saying.
- Display an air of confidence even if you are afraid. Visualize success, believe it will happen.
- Posture is very important as it evokes confidence. It also helps you breathe calmly. Do not lean on things as this loses you 50 percent of your authority. Breathe slowly and evenly. Roll your shoulders back, lifting your chin slightly.
- Speak naturally, like a human being. Speak to the back of the room to ensure that you are heard. Avoid ending your sentences with a questioning tone, this makes you sound unsure of yourself. Instead, make sure that all your sentences are statements.
- Be quick-witted and change direction if the audience is not with you. Scan and read the audience. This will help you to take your focus off yourself and any inward nerves you may have as you instead begin to look outward!

The Least You Need to Know

1. Nerves are OK and natural. People find slight nerves in a speaker endearing.
2. Stand tall and look the audience in the eye.
3. Keep your hands busy if you're a fidgeter. Keep hands out of pockets.
4. Memorize your first few lines instead of reading your introduction.
5. Breathe, smile, and use humor if you have it well practiced.
6. Speak slowly and clearly and make sure that you can be heard.
7. Use gestures and move around a little.
8. Vary the pace, pitch, and tone of your voice.
9. Record yourself on a device to check your voice and body language.
10. Practice, Practice, Practice!

"Courage is what it takes to stand up and speak; courage is also what it takes to sit down and listen."

Winston Churchill

Breathe

Breathe deeply for almost a minute before facing your audience. Never speak publicly from a chair. Always stand as it allows you to breathe properly. You need to breathe evenly when speaking aloud and taking in slow, deep breaths has a calming effect and exhaling slowly gets rid of anxiety.

Standing straight and tall increases your visual presence, and enables you to breathe calmly, and look your audience in the eye, and encourages you to speak confidently. Keep your head up and shoulders back with hands by your side except when you are making convincing gestures to add emphasis to a point you are making.

Tip – Remember, if you need to point at something, make sure your hand is turned sideways or turned over with your palm upright.

A Word on Your Appearance

Even though you are speaking, the message is, in fact, a visual one. If we look like an expert, we convey the message of an expert. Being well dressed and well groomed shows respect to the audience and gives you additional confidence. Jackets give us authority.

Gestures and Actions

Don't distract by fidgeting. Remember that your audience are not only listening to you but more so, looking at you. Mannerisms and fidgeting can distract from your message. Keep your hands by your side or behind your back.

Resist the urge to:

- Put your hands in your pockets
- Fold your arms over your chest
- Fiddle with your hair or your face
- Clench your fists
- Mumble
- Apologize at any point in the talk
- Read every word verbatim

- Use a joke unless you have it well practiced

Nerves are Natural.

Be positive. Visualize a successful fluent and confident talk. Don't hold a sheet of paper if you feel that your hands will shake. Try to have a podium or even a table to put any notes on. Cue cards are easier to hold in a steady way.

Acknowledge that you're nervous. Most audiences are more endearing to speakers who exhibit a slight amount of nerves as it shows sincerity and concern for the topic. Audiences do want a speaker to deliver confidently and successfully, but most people can relate to a speaker who is a bit nervous.

Adrenaline is the fight or flight hormone. This will naturally surface in your body when you are publicly speaking. If a speaker doesn't have that little bit of excitement or nerves, they probably aren't concerned with their topic or pitch. Those who are a little too relaxed and breeze into a public speaking event can often be surprised by a sudden lack of information or detail. A certain amount of adrenaline can ensure that the speaker takes the task seriously and delivers effectively. This is evident to all audiences.

Waiting in line to speak publicly can make you nervous. If you have a choice, try to speak first. If not, make yourself concentrate on what the speakers before you are saying. Distract yourself from your own thoughts about your own speech.

Repetition is a good tool. Tell the audience what you are going to tell them; then tell them; and at the end remind them of what you told them. When practicing you will be monitoring the pace, tone, pitch, and tempo of your voice, but remember that you will need to increase the volume to be heard at the back of a larger room.

Walk and stand as if you are 100 percent confident, whether your knees are shaking or not. Smile! Get them at hello.

This happened to me at a corporate event where myself and a colleague had to introduce our workshop. I stood up from behind the table and told them clearly and concisely what we would be covering. I used a little humor and they gave a positive reaction. Afterward, my colleague said that she couldn't believe how much my knees were shaking. I knew that the audience wouldn't be seeing my knees, so I concentrated on keeping everything else still!

"There are three things to aim at in public speaking: first, to get into your subject, then to get your subject into yourself, and lastly, to get your subject into the heart of your audience."

Alexander Gregg

Summary

In this chapter, we learned about how to get over the nerves of speaking in public. It is essentially "mind over matter." If we work on appearing confident, it can increase our inner confidence.

- It's OK to be nervous.
- Breathe slowly to calm your nerves.
- Positive, fluid gestures and actions display an air of confidence.

Next Steps?

Now that you're beginning to feel more confident to speak in public, it's time to make sure that you're prepared to persuade and convince your audience with a killer speech or pitch!

Chapter 8:

On Your Feet! Persuasive Speeches

"The success of your presentation will be judged not by the knowledge you send but by what the listener receives."
Lilly Walters

Now that you are comfortable with speaking at meetings and in social settings, it's time to think big. You may get to the point in your career where you will need to address a large crowd or an audience. What does it take to deliver a successful speech?

A successful speech will build a picture in the minds of the audience. You need to know what that picture is and how to create it. Writing and delivering a speech is more difficult than making a PowerPoint presentation, but both can be nerve-wracking.

PowerPoint is covered in Chapter 9. But it's better to learn how to make a convincing speech without the crutch of a PowerPoint presentation. You're still a speaker when presenting with slides. For now, we will focus on the speaking part.

A speech is a message from you and it's all about your words, your voice, your dress, and possibly a prop or a display. You want to capture the audience's attention through your words and your connection to them.

Always dress similarly to the audience, this shows respect and professionalism. If there are several speakers, choose to speak first if you have the choice and if possible, chat to a few people beforehand so that you can rely on a few friendly faces and smiles as you start your speech.

The Least You Need to Know

You need to structure your speech so that it has a beginning, middle, and end. Think of a speech as a sandwich, the filling being the largest part of the speech. The beginning and end are smaller components but are more important as they need to enthusiastically convince the audience of your main message. The beginning is the attention grabber. Get them at hello!

The middle contains more detail and is less emotional with more detail and facts. Get them at the introduction and they'll listen to the middle. Then send them off happy, informed, and even wanting more.

First, create bullet point notes for your speech. Start by asking yourself the questions that follow below. Then, string your bullet points into sentences and then let the sentences flow into each other. They form your speaking notes.

- What is my message?
- What do I want the audience to hear and believe?
- What stories can I tell to get my message across?
- Can I start with a story or a question?
- Have I got my facts and details right?
- Have I timed the pitch correctly?
- Can I combine facts with some humor?
- Do I need a suitable prop or display to show the audience?

Speaking Notes

Prepare your notes well and practice reading them out loud many times in advance. Record your speech and listen back and make changes as you see fit. If you prepare well, you will be confident that you have a good speech to deliver successfully.

If you think your hands may shake, make sure in advance that there is a podium or a table to place your notes on. Your notes are one tool other than yourself to deliver a great speech.

Prepare a final set of notes for yourself and make sure that they are legible to you, using one side of the paper only. Number the pages and add color-coding or your own markings and symbols to remind you where and when to emphasize words and use pauses.

Enthusiasm is contagious, so smile while making your speech. Choose a person at the back of the room to speak to and ensure that your volume is correct. Make sure to have water available to you.

Get off to a good start and that's half the battle. Prepare the opening part of your speech and practice, practice, practice. Memorize your opening lines so that you can look more at the audience at the beginning of your speech. This will steady your nerves.

Beginning of a Speech: Grab Their Attention

Grab the attention of the audience by considering some of the following:

- Surprise them with something they do not know, maybe something dramatic.
- Ask them an open-ended question to get them thinking.
- Remind them of something which they already know but emphasize its importance.
- Tell them a story.
- Quote something or someone.
- Tell the audience what they will get out of the talk.
- Build a picture in the mind of the audience.
- Use a prop if appropriate.
- Show your passion for the topic.

Build a rapport early on by using a conversational tone while speaking to the audience. Build common ground by referring to a common experience using the word "we." Tell a relatable story and link the situation or possible experience with that of the audience. In other words, show that you are "one of them" by how you're dressed and by what you say.

Middle of a Speech: Draw the Audience in to Convince Them of Your Message

The middle part is the meat of the sandwich, the main and longest section of the speech. This is where you embellish points from the beginning to develop the message with more detail.

- Know what you are talking about.
- Prepare facts, statistics, and concrete information.
- Use plain language.
- Maintain the attention of the audience and develop interest through enthusiasm and gestures.
- Keep your voice varied in pitch, pace, and tone. Don't go into a monologue, even when delivering a serious set of facts.

Do not bore the audience into restlessness. (I always told my pre-service teachers in lectures that it was up to them to keep their pupils interested as bored pupils can become bold!) Monitor your audience by watching and listening for any signs about how your audience is reacting. Be quick-witted and change direction if need be.

A good method is to go back to a strong point from your opening section. Reminders are good and keep everyone focused. You can recover by reminding them of a point that was received well at the beginning of the speech.

Ending of the Speech

Lead into the end, letting your audience know that you're going to finish on time. This keeps them listening and engaged, almost wanting more.

- Finish on a high note.
- Remind them of your passion for the topic.
- Memorize the ending just as you memorized your opening lines. Use another story or quote. The opening and ending serve as bookends for the main message. They should complement each other in points and tone.
- Briefly summarize and repeat the main points of your speech.
- Say “thank you” and add one last point or phrase.

Leave the audience feeling informed and enlightened. Sometimes people feel very positive toward you when you not only finish on time, but five minutes early.

“They may forget what you said, but they will never forget how you made them feel.”

Carl W. Buechner

Summary

In this chapter, we learned about the preparation needed to deliver a persuasive speech.

- Speaking notes
- Importance of the beginning – the strong opening section
- The more developed middle part requiring real facts and figures
- The strong and positive ending

Next Steps?

We purposely started with speech making as this is more difficult. When making a speech, there is not really a "crutch" in terms of a slideshow to capture attention, as you only have your notes, your voice, your gestures, actions, and your message. You use the combination of these to conjure up images. PowerPoint makes presenting and delivering a message far more visual and easier. PowerPoint is an excellent tool for adding power to our message.

Chapter 9:

Powerful PowerPoint Presentations

"One seeing is better than a hundred times telling about."
Chinese Proverb

PowerPoint is an excellent tool when used properly. With it, you can present your ideas or message using images, diagrams, and graphics within the presentation to inform or persuade your audience of something. The digital "slide show" you create with PowerPoint should work in tandem with your speech.

Through words and images, your goal is to entertain the audience as you inform. Personal stories and even a relevant photo of yourself can help. The fuller a room is, the more engaged an audience will be. If you feel confident enough, ask people to move to the empty seats in the front or if possible, move away from the stage or podium and stand closer to the body of the group and project your voice. Of course, this may not always work if a microphone is fixed to a podium or podium. But if your voice is strong enough to carry without a microphone, do move away and closer to the audience.

PowerPoint slides are generally projected onto a large screen, so use a large font and avoid crowding slides with too much text. Text on slides is just a series of prompts for your verbal delivery of the message. The slides are like your cue cards for a speech. Too much text will stop the audience from listening to you as they will automatically read all the text before focusing on you and your voice. The text should be bullet points that you expand upon with your speech. Otherwise, it comes across as you just reading aloud.

Use animated body language and gestures to match the message you are projecting. Start strong and finish strong. Begin by saying that you will take any questions at the end. That way, you won't be distracted or interrupted during the presentation, which can ruin the flow of your message.

Use approximately ten slides but have extras if you feel that you may be asked for more detail. Remember: Less is more!

The Least You Need to Know

P – Pictures and props are as good as text

O – Open the presentation with a question and or a story

W – Watch the audience for reactions

E – Ensure that your hands are not clenched or in pockets

R – Repeat important messages

P – Prepare extra slides in case you need them

O – Organize a beginning, middle, and end

I – Inspirational quotes are useful

N – Notes are important but try not to read your speech word-for-word

T – Timing is everything: finish on time. Leave enough time for questions

PowerPoint Tips

- As with delivering a pitch, focus on the message. Research your topic and organize a sequence of slides to deliver your message.
- Use quotations, facts, and statistics. Keep the content simple using diagrams or graphs and charts instead of too many figures. It's easier to see a bar graph or pie chart from afar than it is to keep track of columns of numbers.
- Restrict the amount of information and the number of words on each slide. These are prompts for you to embellish with a further message.
- Make sure that each of your slides has the same main heading and or logo to keep the brand and message continuously visible.
- Props and visual aids add even more images to your message but use them wisely. Balance the use of pictures on slides and objects that you can hold to enhance your message.
- Keep to the time limit. If you finish on time or even five minutes early, your audience will be positive toward you and remember your presentation favorably.
- Incorporate a Questions and Answers session within the time limit. This is your last slide which says, "Thank you."

Body Language of a Good Presenter

Your slides need to be captivating, but so do you. Don't count on the slides alone to keep the audience's attention. As with other public speaking opportunities, make sure you remember your body language and use it to connect to the audience.

Stand up straight. Don't lean on things. Look alert. Keep a balance between standing upright and moving slightly. Use gestures. Use eye contact, scanning the room slowly as you speak. Smile.

Keep your hands busy if they might get you into trouble by clenching them or putting them in your pockets. Hold something such as a prop or a pen. Rest your hands on a podium or a table where your props are. Gently holding your hands behind your back is acceptable also.

Resting your hands on something is more powerful than leaning on something which can diminish your presence. Resting is done with your hands but leaning with your elbow or shoulder looks very casual and less powerful and should be avoided.

Your voice is an important part of your delivery. Make sure that you can be heard at the back of the room. Vary the pitch, pace, and tone of your voice at times for emphasis.

Remember that as your audience is hearing your message for the first time, it must be delivered clearly and slower than your usual conversational voice.

If you have a joke to tell, make sure it is well rehearsed.

"By failing to prepare, you are preparing to fail."
Benjamin Franklin

Prepare and Practice

Preparation is the key to the success of your presentation and can give you more confidence. Practice is just as important. Be positive and visualize success. Make sure that your slides are legible at the back of the room.

Anticipate potential technical hiccups. Check all electrical and audiovisual equipment in advance. Make sure to have a backup of your slides and a printed-out version of the slides for yourself to keep you on track.

This happened to me when delivering a BizWorld workshop to the children of staff from a sponsoring bank during their midterm. The cable of my laptop wasn't compatible to the old projector and screen, so I had to "visually" speak my slides to the children. I was so prepared that I could walk them through the slides as I could see them clearly in my own head!

Aim to be ready before your audience enters the room with your first slide on the screen. However, if the occasion dictates that you must walk to the front of the room, make sure that you are holding your notes clearly and confidently. Avoid racing through the room shuffling notes in your hand. Remember that the audience is sizing you and your message up, even before you speak.

Don't be afraid to invite the audience to ask you questions at the end. Repeat the question back to the person to make sure that you have heard it correctly. Not only will this buy you time to consider your answer, but it also allows the rest of the audience to hear the question clearly. Answer the question as honestly as you can. It's okay to admit if you don't know the complete answer to every aspect of the question. Tell the person that you will investigate and follow up with them in a day or two.

Tips for Presenting

- Be clear
- Once you have settled your nerves, move away from the podium
- Own the stage—move around a little
- Use gestures and body language to emphasize your message
- Use a famous inspirational quote
- Pause for emphasis of an important point
- Stress words that are part of the key message
- Vary the tone, tempo, pace, and pitch of your voice
- If you are interesting, the audience will be interested
- Scan the room and be aware of the audience
- Change direction if your message is not reaching the audience

Summary

In this chapter, we learned about how PowerPoint can add power to a speech and our message using the following:

- Pictures
- Inspirational Quotes
- Props
- Timing
- Body Language and Gestures
- Voice

Next Steps?

People hear you when you communicate through speeches and presentations.

The written word is another form of your personal and public communication. Correct spelling and punctuation can ensure that your written message gives a good impression.

Did you know that spell-check on your smartphone, tablet, or laptop can miss incorrect usage of words in certain contexts?

Read on to find out what these words are and how to beat the spell-checkers!

Chapter 10:

Skills in Writing—Spell-Check isn't Always Right

The English language is full of contradictions and traps. Just consider the words "heart," "heard," and "beard." Each contains e-a-r, and each is pronounced differently. Spelling can be just as complicated. Most word processing programs have an internal spell-checker, but how much can you rely on it?

You need to have correct spelling to impress in writing all text for pitches, letters, business plans, speeches, presentations, or emails. While you can use spell-check, MS Editor function, or software like Grammarly, there are still words that may be spelled correctly but used incorrectly.

Spell-check misses many words called homophones. Homophones are words that are pronounced and sound the same but are spelled differently and have different meanings. Not knowing these could let your professionalism down through the written word.

The Least You Need to Know

Most common misused words:

To Too Two

There Their They're

Lose Loose

Principal Principle

Using Contractions

You don't have to crack open a big grammar book to sound professional but be careful with your verb tenses. While a lot of phrases are common in casual usage, you should steer away from being too casual in your written communication. Be mindful of the level of formality at your workplace. Even a contraction (using an apostrophe as in "I've" to mean "I have,") could be considered too familiar or unprofessional. Many large companies have a style guide for their written material and correspondence. If this applies to your workplace, please make sure you use it in your emails and such.

All the phrases below are correct:

I took – I have taken – I've taken

I did – I have done – I've done

I went – I have gone – I've gone

I wrote – I have written – I've written

I ate – I have eaten – I've eaten

I was – I have been – I've been

Never say, "I done it," or "I seen it."

Top Tip: Do not overuse contractions. You are better off using one per sentence. For instance: "We'd better hurry because I've got an event I'd better not miss and don't want to be late." All of these contractions make the sentence choppy. Be aware that the contraction "I'd" could be misread as "I had," "I would," or "I should," and spell out each phrase if there is ambiguity or confusion.

Fun Homophone Quiz

Take this fun quiz to check your use of homophones in sentences. Circle the correct word option and try to think of a sentence in your head for the other incorrect option. This will aid you to remember the difference between the two words – the two homophones.

The Answer key is below.

Each of the statements below have right and wrong options for homophones. Circle the word that you think is correct.

Answers are below.

1. At Christmas time everyone tends to ___too much.

bye buy by

2. I hope that you are enjoying this ___ game.

bored board

3. It is best to speak clearly so that people can ___ you.

here hear

4. The word ___ is often used at the beginning of a question.

witch which

5. It is lovely to walk on a beach in your ___ feet.

bare bear

6. Every shoe has a sole and a ___.

heal heel

7. After school I will hopefully take a ___ in the subject that I like the best.

course coarse

8. After being ill, one usually feels ___.

week weak

9. When leaving people, we tend to say ___

bye by buy

10. Bricks and cement are found on a building ___.

sight site

11. A severe cold is often referred to as a ___.

flew flu

12. In autumn, we often look at the leaves on the ___tree.

beach beech

13. I need to buy a Birthday gift for my ___.

son sun

14. Shoelaces are used to tie a ___.

not knot

15. One must be patient when one must ____ a long time.

weight wait

16. We are always looking forward to a summer ___ from work or school.

brake break

17. You need to speak up so that you can be ___.

herd heard

18. Trees produce ___ for making objects such as furniture.

would wood

19. When in a queue, one must be prepared to ___.

wait weight

20. ___ many people are nervous of making presentations.

To Too Two

21. One of the ingredients in a cake is usually ____.

flower flour

22. Many yachts usually have a ___.

sale sail

23. The headteacher who runs a school is called the ____.

principle principal

24. To enter a room, one must walk ___ a doorway.

through threw

25. When something rises, such as prices, it can be said to ___.

soar sore

26. The part of every plant that is underground is usually called the ___.

route root

27. A bird that kills other animals for food is often referred to as a bird of ___.

pray prey

28. ____ are all going on holidays soon.

There Their They're

29. Fish eaters often like to eat ___.

sole soul

30. A job in a company or a part in a play can be referred to as a ___.

role roll

31. ___ are twenty-six letters in the alphabet.

There Their They're

32. People who like red meat often like to eat ___.

steak stake

33. To stitch fabric together is to ___.

sow sew

34. People often need to ___ out clothes when they get wet.

ring wring

35. Shoes and socks always come in a ___.

pair pear

36. A ___ is another word for a story.

tale tail

37. A number of hotel rooms combined is often called a ___.

suite sweet

38. It is rude to stop and ___ at people.

stair stare

39. There is a ___ way to do something and a wrong way.

write right

40. Hospitals take care of many ___.

patience patients

41. It is not good to ___ in other people's business.

medal meddle

42. We were ___ many subjects in school.

taught thought

43. Many metal objects are made of ____.

steel steal

44. Every window has at least one ___ of glass.

pain pane

45. To ___ is to remove the skin from a fruit.

peal peel

46. It is advisable to memorize the ___ points of your presentation.

mane main

47. The guests need to bring ___ suitcases.

there their they're

48. It is important to shake hands when you ___ someone for the first time.

meat meet

49. When something is inexpensive it is often referred to as ___.

cheap cheep

50. Opinionated people can often think they are always ___.

write right

51. It is often nice to be offered a ___ of cake.

peace piece

52. W.B. Yeats said: "Education is not the filling of a ___ but the lighting of a fire."

pale pail

53. A person who inherits something is called an ___.

heir air

54. It is important not to ___ your smartphone.

lose loose

Answers:

1. buy, 2. board, 3. hear, 4. which, 5. bare, 6. heel,

7. course, 8. weak, 9. bye, 10. site, 11. flu, 12. beech

13. son, 14. knot, 15. wait, 16. break, 17. heard, 18. wood,

19. wait, 20. Too, 21. flour, 22. sail, 23. principal, 24. through,

25. soar, 26. root, 27. prey, 28 They're, 29. sole, 30. role,

31. There, 32. steak, 33. sew, 34. wring, 35. pair, 36. tale,

37. suite, 38. stare, 39. right, 40. patients, 41. meddle, 42. taught,

43. steel, 44. pane, 45. peel, 46. main, 47. their, 48. meet,

49. cheap, 50. right, 51. piece, 52. pail, 53. heir, 54. lose

There are many more examples of homophones online. If this is an area of difficulty for you, Google search online quizzes and practice. Seeing examples and quizzing yourself is the easiest way to see the words used correctly in context rather than memorizing lists of words. Being familiar with homophones will greatly improve your writing and your confidence.

Summary

In this chapter, we learned about the words that can escape spell check. These are called homophones.

- Homophones are words that sound the same but have a different meaning.
- Homophones are words that are spelled correctly but are used incorrectly due to the context of the sentence.
- Because they are not spelled incorrectly, spell check software may not alert you to this misuse of the word.

You have now completed the first two parts of this book! Let's pause for a minute and look at some ways to improve your life and confidence in small and big ways.

10 Simple Steps to Success

1. Buy yourself a nice pen and notebook.
2. Do not try to change your accent. Accents are charming as long as they are understood.
3. Learn to cook at least one dish.
4. Read some real news, preferably off-line.
5. Read a book—it makes you a more interesting conversationalist.
6. Have a go at learning a new language. There are many free apps out there for learning a language.
7. Cultivate your talents and or learn a new skill. It gives you more to talk about and you will connect with people.
8. Learn how to write a handwritten letter, how to fold a letter properly into an envelope, and how to address an envelope correctly.
9. Practice your people skills; they are just as important as your academic skills.
10. Good manners and a smile will open any door. Say "thank you" for small things like someone holding the door for you.
11. Have a goal in life, no matter how small!
12. Don't be afraid to try something new. Failures are the best way to learn. Have a go!

Post a letter to yourself. Yes, physically write yourself a letter, address the envelope to yourself, put a stamp on it, and post it to yourself. Enjoy receiving, opening, and reading a letter, written especially for you.

Next Steps?

The next part of *Career Elevator* is called "I'm an Entrepreneur, Now What?"

Don't stop reading yet. You have an understanding of success and you know how to influence others and promote yourself within an organization.

You will learn about the four types of entrepreneurs:

- Intrapreneurs
- Policy Entrepreneurs
- Social Entrepreneurs
- Traditional Entrepreneurs

So, you can be innovative whether you work with people, for people, for an organization, or for yourself.

PART THREE: I'M AN ENTREPRENEUR, NOW WHAT?

Featuring:

Section A: All About You as an Entrepreneur

Section B: All About You Starting a Business

Section C: All About You Pitching Your Business and Forming a Team

Section A:

All About You as an Entrepreneur

Well done on your success in getting this far in the book. Success means that you are an all-rounder, that you've achieved a lot personally and professionally.

But it doesn't mean you're finished learning. Be a lifelong learner—Never stop learning. No person or organization can improve and advance if they stop trying new things, fixing problems, and increasing their knowledge.

Success also means that you are aware of improvements that can be made. Becoming aware of how you can make a difference is all about resilience.

Entrepreneurs see opportunities to improve and turn an idea into a business. You will be practicing all the skills learned in "You're Hired" and "To Promotion and Beyond" should you choose to give entrepreneurship a go.

We often learn more from failure than from success. Before inventing the lightbulb, Thomas Edison didn't regard any of his previous attempts as failures, saying, "I just found 10,000 ways that didn't work."

Therefore, you need perseverance. You need to keep at it and know when to pivot and change direction. You also need the patience to see the big picture and the long-term goal. Goals are very important at this stage. Are they SMART?

"The important thing is to dare to dream big, then take action to make it come true."

Joe Girard

Chapter 1:

Innovation from Trial and Error

"Develop success from failure. Discouragement and failure are two of the surest stepping stones to success."

Dale Carnegie

Do you remember the new meaning that we gave to the acronym MBA? This new interpretation of the letters will launch us into this section:

M Making

B Business

A An Adventure

Innovating and creating a business out of an idea is very exciting. It's an adventure. Adventures are not all smooth sailing. It is a constant cycle of trials and errors. Failures are part of the journey and we learn from failures and try again.

You may be familiar with Dyson vacuums and products. Did you know those innovations were borne from failure? James Dyson is a great example of never giving up. He successfully created a vacuum machine with no vacuum bag and no loss of suction. It took him five years and 5,127 prototypes. James and his team of engineers are always improving Dyson technology. They never stop learning, adapting, and improving.

"This defines entrepreneur and entrepreneurship - The entrepreneur always searches for change, responds to it, and exploits it as an opportunity."

Peter Drucker

Peter Drucker is frequently referred to as the father of innovation. According to Drucker, innovation is not invention, but doing something different. He suggested that innovations be simple, small, focused, and successful. His definition of innovation is "doing things differently and doing things better."

Essentially, it is solving a problem and making a change for the better with what already exists. Jeb Blount, author and speaker who helps people reach their full potential, really summed up the purpose of a business: "The essence of business is one person solving another person's problem." Entrepreneurs are constantly on the lookout for problems they can solve. They look for patterns and make connections.

Do you see a gap in the marketplace or the need for a new product? Just look at the pandemic. Who knew meal delivery services would be a must for many people around the globe? By looking at what works and doesn't work well, you may have the solution to a problem.

The Least You Need to Know

- Many types of Entrepreneurs exist.
- Anyone can be an innovator.
- You don't just have to own and run your own business to be innovative.
- One can also be an intrapreneur working in a business or company.
- One can be a social entrepreneur by setting up a not-for-profit initiative.
- One can also be a policy entrepreneur while employed at an agency or company.
- Innovators ask questions. They are not afraid to disrupt the norms.
- To have an innovative idea in mind, you need to have goals.
- Your goals need to be SMART:

Specific

Measurable

Achievable

Realistic

Time-bound

"If you always do what you've always done, you'll always get what you've always got."

Henry Ford

Why do People Fear Failure?

Is the fear of failure educated in us or part of human nature?

Is childlike wonder and creativity educated out of us as we grow and are steered toward practical paths?

Picasso said, "We're all born artists – it's just educated out of us."

School curricula and teaching favor hard skills. In many countries, mandated standardized testing focuses schools on only IQ, memorizing knowledge, and getting good grades. But what about the other skills like communication, team building, collaboration, negotiation, and presenting? These are not just invaluable "soft skills," they are universal life skills that will help any child become a more confident person and capable member of society.

Teachers often find that their hands are tied as there aren't enough hours in the day to foster soft skills into their classes. As a teacher, I strove to encourage pupils to ask questions and seek problems to empower them to seek solutions for themselves. I had to remind myself not to give pupils the answers to questions. Sometimes you learn more from a "wrong" answer than you do from being right the first time. Unfortunately, teachers don't always have time to move beyond the constraints of the curriculum.

One thing teachers can do is to incorporate soft skills within the framework of the subject matter. By having students read aloud, give short presentations, and work in teams, the children are learning way more than they would just through reading and testing. Just being in school prepares a child for dealing with all kinds of people in the world, but by making small changes in the classroom, you are essentially teaching public speaking, writing a presentation, and teamwork, as the students learn the subject.

"Ever tried. Ever failed. No matter. Try again. Fail again. Fail better."

Samuel Beckett

Paralysis from Failure

Fear of failure can paralyze your progress. The phrase "paralysis from analysis" is about spending too much time going over every single outcome and problem that may arise and never really taking action. It is wise to do this, but don't be afraid to jump in and "have a go." The secret to success is to learn from failure. Innovation is always churning out new products and systems. The current automation threat requires us to be less risk-averse and try out new skills to keep up with progress. Hard skills are fixed but soft skills are flexible and agile. There is always room to flex those soft skills.

What's Wrong with the F Word?

Why does education fear failure?

Do teachers fear that it will reflect on them?

Educators fearing failure can stifle innovation and creativity.

Teachers need to be given the freedom to allow for failure and constant discovery learning. There needs to be an acknowledgment that the teacher no longer needs to be the font of all knowledge. They shouldn't be perceived as having all the answers, but given the freedom to encourage and inspire students to seek out knowledge themselves.

Knowledge is available ubiquitously at the click of a mouse and freely available on most platforms. Teachers, pupils, and schools need to be given access to the best form of technology to access this knowledge for themselves. After all, it's what a pupil does with the knowledge that's important. Rather than "recalling" knowledge only for memory's sake, pupils can be encouraged to understand, apply, analyze, create, and evaluate knowledge. That way pupils become active in their own learning.

I lectured math competency to pre-service teachers. I am passionate about numbers and I enjoyed breaking down the concepts and enlightening them on the basics of math so that they could confidently teach math to their own pupils. I have an ex-student who remains a friend and she said that when she was teaching math to her pupils, she would hear my voice in her head.

She told me that I was so passionate about teaching that "you could smell the chalk off you!" These were her exact words! That sticks with me because this is the passion that I know most teachers have. They want to engage, inspire, and educate their students. Let's give teachers the freedom to do just that by addressing the constraints of over-testing.

As William Butler Yeats said, **"Education is not the filling of a pail, but the lighting of a fire."** It is ineffective education to concentrate primarily on filling a pail without "igniting" interest in the student to engage with learning themselves.

How to Learn to Fail for Successful Creativity

This is what needs to be learned. Failures lead to Flexibility which leads to new Future possibilities.

- Learn by doing
- Learn by experience
- Learn by reflecting on failures
- Apply new knowledge based on this learning

"The true sign of intelligence is not knowledge but imagination."
Albert Einstein

Learning through Creativity

I used to love seeing my kids make something new out of LEGO after they had initially stuck to the instructions for creating a step-by-step Harry Potter room in Hogwarts. They got more enjoyment out of breaking up the original project and making their own version. They were able to "tell me the story" of what was in the rooms they designed. This small exercise gave them many more opportunities to be creative.

When you let your mind wonder, question, imagine, and play with ideas, you can be truly innovative. To play more is to create more.

Anyone who has been around small children has noticed that they get more fun playing with the box than with the toy that came in it. That is because a toy can just require passive play, like following a guideline based on what the toy does. However, when kids use an empty box for imaginative play, this is active play and it opens endless possibilities.

According to Dr. Rene Tristan, CEO of LEGO Education Europe, "To create is human – children enjoy solving problems and are wired to take on challenging tasks."

As CEO of BizWorld, creativity was encouraged in school children with no prior knowledge of innovation or business. We achieved this by offering schools a workshop program complementary to the existing curriculum. We facilitated this learning through the provision of the opportunities for pupils to:

Investigate

Discover

Discuss

Imagine

Play

Innovating is simply making a change for the better. Learning and improving through failures is the path to innovation.

Encourage Curiosity

I was a Froebel trained teacher in the '80s. Two phrases that remained with me in all my working life were:

- Never do for a child what they can do for themselves.
- Never tell a child something that they can find out for themselves.

I adopted this all my teaching life and also for my parenting style. I raised two independent sons. This book is about active learning, working on yourself. Learn by doing and take it in steps.

Subjects in textbooks could be dry and boring and were difficult to teach and make interesting for pupils. After introducing the topic to pupils, I split the class into three groups. One group created their own word searches on the topic, another group collaborated in pairs to create a simple crossword on the topic, the last group wrote out table quiz questions (with the answers). Friday was activity day and the word searches and crosswords were photocopied and passed around so every pupil had an activity to do. Then we had a class table quiz on the topic using the questions the pupils developed. These activity preparations had the pupils reading and re-reading the textbook to create the word searches, crosswords, and quiz questions. They were learning unknown to themselves.

They were also learning how to figure out the key points to a topic, how to work as a team, how to create puzzles and quizzes, and, in doing so, create fun activities that they could share with their fellow students. It was rewarding to see the sense of accomplishment and ownership on the part of the pupils. Learning the subject matter just came more naturally as part of a larger project.

Action Step:

Listen to Dr. Ken Robinson's Ted Talk called "Schools Kill Creativity."

Summary

In this chapter, we learned about how anyone can be an entrepreneur no matter what their situation.

- Many types of entrepreneurs exist
- Innovators ask questions and their goals are SMART
- Failure is not to be feared
- Failures are learning opportunities
- Learning and teaching are opportunities for creative success and innovation

Next Steps?

An entrepreneurial mindset is a culmination of many of the skills covered already in this book. The confidence developed so far enables you to look for problems and consider solutions for everyday problems for everyday people. Read on to find out what drives entrepreneurs.

Chapter 2:

What IS an Entrepreneur?

"Learn from yesterday, live for today, hope for tomorrow. The important thing is to not stop questioning."
Albert Einstein

Entrepreneurs are keenly aware of themselves and the world around them. They are experts at soft skills and don't get hung up on hard skills.

They ask questions, look for problems, and strive to offer solutions. They are curious.

Entrepreneurs are not afraid to have a go and keep learning. They don't fear failure—they know that they'll learn from it. They know that a successful business will earn them money, but their primary motivation is to solve a problem. First and foremost, they have a subjective reason to start a business.

"Happiness is not in the mere possession of money; it lies in the joy of achievement, in the thrill of creative effort."
Franklin D. Roosevelt

The Least You Need to Know

Entrepreneurs come in all shapes and sizes, but they share certain characteristics and skills.

Entrepreneurial Characteristics

Creative

Innovative

Calculated risk-taker

Confident in one's ability

Resilient

Hard-working

Flexible

Decisive

Motivated

Entrepreneurial Skills

Goal Setting

People Management

Delegation

Inner Control

Self-Management

Reality Perception

Entrepreneurs know and believe that there is more to life than IQ. They know that multiple kinds of intelligence exist. Knowledge is IQ. These are hard skills run by the left side of our brain.

But what about the right side of our brain?

In his book, *A Whole New Mind: Why Right-Brainers Will Rule the Future,* author Daniel Pink advocated for bridging the gap between the left and right sides of our brain to allow us to wonder and create. He suggests that we all need to learn how to use our right brains as the "future belongs to creators, empathizers, pattern recognizers and meaning makers." He talks about the value of "traditionally neglected talents" that are underestimated in the business world, but crucial to success. Remember that your EQ and people skills are a different kind of smart.

Entrepreneurs have a high EQ level and place a high value on **PEOPLE** skills. They know and believe that people skills are strategy skills. They know and believe that people skills are business skills.

P – Personal awareness

E - Emotional awareness

O - Optimism

P - Personality

L – Listening and speaking

E – Ethics and Etiquette (Good old-fashioned manners!)

Daniel Goleman's book, *Emotional Intelligence: Why it Can Matter More Than IQ,* refers to numerous studies of corporations to assess what capabilities were favored and vital for success. "Emotional competencies such as trustworthiness, adaptability and a talent for collaboration," were common to many successful organizations. He mentions "communication skills, interpersonal skills, and initiative," as essential elements of EQ.

He lists teamwork, confidence, optimism, empathy, and problem solving, as emotional competencies. These are all characteristics of a successful entrepreneur and having these qualities—plus curiosity—leads to innovation.

Goleman puts a high value on empathy. Remember when we talked about listening more than you speak? This is one part of empathy. It is trying to understand others' feelings and *wanting* to understand others. When you have insight into another person's personality and motivations, you can use different methods of communication and incentives that may work better with that person and lead to more cooperation.

Here is a good phrase to remember what SOFT skills can help you accomplish:

SOFT SKILLS

S Successful people

O Overcome

F Failure &

T Try again

These soft skills enable people to put **DRIVE** into action:

D Determination

R Resilience

I Innovation

V Vision

E Enthusiasm

Action Steps:

Look at the acrostic phrases above and the lists of entrepreneurial characteristics. Ask yourself these questions:

- Can you identify yourself in any of these?
- Could you see yourself "having a go" and cultivating any of them?
- Can you open your mind to the fact that problems exist all around us which could be solved?

Remember: Be kind to yourself. Developing resilience and an entrepreneurial mindset doesn't happen overnight—and it's not easy.

Summary

In this chapter, we learned about how entrepreneurs have and develop a certain skill set that leads to drive and motivation:

- Entrepreneurial Characteristics
- Entrepreneurial Skills
- PEOPLE skills
- SOFT skills
- DRIVE

Next Steps?

Now that we know more about what drives an entrepreneur, it's natural to ask: How do these people find opportunities to be entrepreneurial? Simply put, they're not afraid to look for problems. And they get excited thinking about solutions for these problems. Entrepreneurs don't just wait for opportunities to fall into their laps. They create opportunities by looking for problems.

Chapter 3:

How to Look for Problems

"Let's go invent tomorrow instead of worrying about what happened yesterday."

Steve Jobs

The aim of all businesses is to solve a problem. Problems are just opportunities to be creative. Just look at Steve Jobs and how the smartphone changed the way we communicate, collaborate, and cooperate. How did this one innovation solve the problem of lack of connectivity in a global marketplace?

The business world is full of innovators who solve problems for other people. They use their full range of soft skills to connect with people to find out what problems people have. This enables them to be in tune with others and acutely aware. They know that people want their problems solved and that people will pay for a solution.

Looking for problems starts with you. What's your passion? What topic absorbs your thoughts and mind? What do you find yourself reading and talking about? Many people turn a hobby into a real business. Your own experience is your first resource as an entrepreneur. There is wealth and value in your own personal experience and talents.

The Least You Need to Know

Think about how you live. What you do every day. Think about a few things that you wish could be better. Ask yourself these questions:

What do you hear others complaining about?

What do you find yourself complaining about?

Is it:

- Somewhere you go to.
- Something you do.
- Something you use.
- Or something else.

Can you think of an idea to:

- Make life healthier for people.
- Make life quicker for people.
- Make life simpler for people.
- Make life safer for people.
- Make life nicer for people.
- Improve the lives of certain people.
- Empower the lives of certain people.

Action One:

Think about how you live, what interests you, and what you love doing. Could some aspect of your day-to-day activities be improved?

Brainstorm and fill a page with whatever thoughts and ideas come into your head. This is a "mind map." Just keep writing words and phrases and topics. Can they be grouped?

Open your mind and just keep writing until you have nothing left in your head. You will enjoy this exercise as it will be about a topic that you're passionate about. You can also move beyond your own personal experience by opening your mind to the world of others.

"We can't solve problems by using the same kind of thinking we used when we created them."

Albert Einstein

Possible Issues to Tackle

This is like doing field research. For now, explore the world around you to look for problems. It can be as close as in your home, to the wider community, or to the world. There is a multitude of issues facing us which have associated problems and could benefit from better solutions.

Below is a small sample to prompt you:

Recycling issues

Water conversation issues

Gardening issues

Pet ownership issues

Caring for other people issues

Technology issues

Road safety and transport issues

Mindfulness issues

Homelessness issues

Food waste issues

Employment issues

Nutrition issues

Education issues

The World's Sustainable Development Goals were launched by the United Nations in 2015. They are a list of seventeen connected objectives designed to create a better world for all by 2030.

Read the list below. If you want to stretch yourself, try to think of an idea to raise awareness, educate people, or provide a solution to any of the following sustainable development goals.

1. No poverty
2. No hunger
3. Good health
4. Quality education
5. Gender equality
6. Clean water and sanitation
7. Renewable energy
8. Good jobs and economic growth
9. Innovation and infrastructure
10. Reduced inequalities
11. Sustainable cities and communities
12. Responsible consumption

13. Climate action
14. Life below water
15. Life on land
16. Peace and justice
17. Partnerships for the goals

For now, just open your mind and imagine what problems you could provide a solution for, whether it be a product, a service, or both. Don't be afraid to let your imagination fly. Your idea could solve a small problem for many people or solve a large problem for the planet.

Action Two:

Keep adding to your mind map as ideas come into your head.

The next section helps you develop an idea into a business. Hopefully, you will have too many ideas at this stage. Let your mind reflect on these. Take time and open your mind.

Don't forget that it's an adventure.

Summary

In this chapter, we learned about how simple everyday problems can offer opportunities for innovators to offer solutions.

- Look for problems close to home.
- Look for problems others may have.
- The Worlds Sustainable Development Goals cover problems that people have globally.

Next Steps?

A business idea starts with a problem and, in turn, a solution. This becomes a real business when you have customers to pay for your solution. This can be a product, a service, or both.

Read on.

Section B:

All About You Starting a Business

In this section, we cover the basics of starting a business. It can be an exciting, yet frustrating challenge to start something from scratch. How do you pay for your start-up business? How do you write a business plan?

We will look at all of those aspects and more.

Chapter 4:

How to Start a Business

"Only those who will risk going too far can possibly find out how far one can go."

T.S. Elliot

Starting a business is an adventure. It takes courage as it is both exciting and daunting at the same time. A new business, known as a start-up, is not a quick-fix solution to a problem. It involves a lot of planning and mistakes will be made along the way.

Think back on the skills and characteristics of entrepreneurs. Starting a business is not easy. but becoming an entrepreneur will mean that you will not let failures discourage you. It's a journey and you'll learn from mistakes as you perfect your business model and methods.

The Least You Need to Know

Identify the problem that your business can provide a solution for. Ask yourself the following questions:

- Why are you solving this problem?
- What are you doing to solve this problem?
- What's your USP?
- Who will be your customers be?
- How will you reach your customers?

Your business can either sell a product, or a service, or both.

The Profit Equation

Revenue – Expenses = Profit.

All businesses need a revenue stream. Even charities and not-for-profit initiatives need a revenue stream to be sustainable. There are many costs associated with running a business and they all must be paid before any revenue from sales can be called a profit. Expenses are often called "overhead." That would include rent, advertising, buying products or goods, and employees. The lower your expenses, the higher your profit.

There are different types of businesses:

- If you choose to work on your own, you are a sole trader.
- You may also want to work with someone and create a partnership.
- You may want to employ others with the skills the business needs and form a company team.

Most businesses are for profit. Not-for-profit groups or organizations differ as they put any profit back into the business once staff, costs, and expenses are paid. These organizations may also have volunteers who are not paid wages, but their expenses are usually paid by the business. This type of business can also be called a social enterprise.

Market Research

So, you have found a problem and you've thought of a solution. But how do you know if others think that this is also a problem? You need to investigate whether others will pay for this solution and, if so, what is the price point? This is market research to find your target audience or customer.

Speak to people, conduct surveys, and do an internet search for similar products or services. You need to know whether people will pay for the solution you're offering to their problem. This is crucial knowledge.

"An investment in knowledge pays interest."
Benjamin Franklin

If you're solving a problem that is related to your own passion, interests, and experience, then you are part of your target market. This makes it easier to research the viability of the business as you're surrounded by your target market frequently. If you know the industry or field, you become a trustworthy source and advocate for your product.

Product or Service

Creating and selling a new product can be difficult and a lengthy process. How will your source raw materials? How expensive will it be to manufacture the product? Will you need legal protection, such as a patent and trademark, to keep others from replicating your product or design?

Selling a service can often be easier as you are selling yourself, your skills, and your experience. You and your expertise become the product. You need to ask yourself if you have a skill that can make life simpler, easier, better, safer, or quicker for people in your target market.

You can start off small by offering your skills yourself as a sole trader. If you want to grow the business, you can train others to provide the same skill to reach more customers. Do you have a "side hustle" as you keep a regular job? Many people grow their small businesses as they continue to work at a full-time job. This is a great way to prove your business model can be successful and determine what works and what doesn't. You can turn your passion into a career while still collecting a regular paycheck.

Below is a small sample of the wide range of skills that you could provide through your business. The possibilities are endless.

- Writing
- Designing
- Programming
- Advertising
- Web development
- Cooking
- Transporting
- Coaching
- Consulting
- Training
- Educating
- Entertaining
- Informing
- Caring
- Marketing
- Guiding
- App development
- Influencing

Influencing is a relatively new phenomenon. This offers a passive income to people who promote other businesses' products or services online and receive a commission on each sale or a fee for promoting the business. It takes a lot of luck to make money as an influencer, so it's best to combine influencing with another skill and build your clientele through videos or how-to information. Are you an expert fisherman or a chef? The more visible you are on social media as you share your story, tips, and training, the closer you are to gaining sponsors and commissions. Anyone can be an influencer, but it won't happen overnight.

Summary

In this chapter, we learned about different business models.

- The Profit Equation
- Finding and reaching out to customers
- Market research

Next Steps?

Writing a business plan is the easiest way to turn your mind map into a structured business idea. How do you distill your ideas into a comprehensive plan? Read on!

Chapter 5:

Creating a Business Plan

A business plan is an overview of your business and can be as detailed as required depending on the business and sector. You will need a well-developed, detailed business plan if you are seeking a bank loan or funding for your business.

A good way to think of a business plan is to visualize it as a pizza with many slices. It contains all the components of the business. Every part is important and impacts on the other components.

The Least You Need to Know

Here is an acrostic to help you think of all of the different aspects of creating a business plan:

B – Business Vision

U – USP: Are there competitors?

S – Solution offered by your business

I – Issue: What is the problem?

N– New innovative proposition

E – Executive team: People in the business

S – Short-term goals

S – Sales Strategy

P – PEST and SWOT Analysis

L – Long-term goals

A – Action required to market the business

N – Name it: The importance of branding

We have already looked at SWOT analysis, but what is PEST?

PEST is an acronym for Political, Economic, Social, and Technological. By taking a look at each of these categories and seeing how they relate to your business, you can create a stronger business plan. PEST analysis helps you determine how these factors will affect the performance and activities of your business in the long term.

Ask yourself these questions. The answers will form your business plan:

- What problem are you solving?
- How are you solving it?
- What have you learned from market research?
- What is your USP?
- Who is your target audience?
- How will you reach your customers?
- Have you any plans for future products?

Branding

Branding is an important aspect of your business and the business plan. Your brand is not only the name of your business, but what it stands for.

It is the message and image that the business communicates to make the consumer feel an affinity with your product or service. Think of your brand as a box of cereal.

What imagery and colors on the cereal box reflect your business? What name and message on the box tell consumers what your business does? What facts and details of your business can you put on the back and the sides of the box? What are the ingredients of your business? What are the benefits of buying from your business?

Strengthen and build your brand daily by the way you do business and the way you behave with existing customers. It is crucial that your reputation in the market reflects your overall brand.

What's in a Name?

Name your business. It can be related specifically to what the business does, or it can be a unique unrelated name. It might contain your own name or letters from names in the partnership or team. It needs to be easy to say, easy to remember, and easy to spell. Remember that your business name needs to be easily searchable in online browsers. It may look cute to call your business "Kourtney Kuts" if your name is Kourtney and you cut hair. But how many famous Kourtneys will come up in searches before you? How will someone find you if they spell "haircut" the traditional way? These are all considerations in the internet age.

If you choose to use a numeral in your business name, you will keep having to correct people who misspell it. Think of a radio ad for your business. When mentioning your business name during the ad, do you have to remind listeners of how to spell it? For instance, if your company is called Treatz 4 Pupz, the ad will always have to say, "that's treatz with a Z … the number four … Pupz with a Z." In the digital age, it will be confusing as potential consumers try to find your website.

Seek feedback from people in your target market regarding the name of the business. Look online to see if others are already using that name or a close variation of it. Search government trademark and patent databases before you settle on a name. Once you are happy with your name, you can register and incorporate your business.

Vision and Mission Statement

You need to set goals for the business. What does your business aim to do and be? Your website and all marketing material must be consistent with your brand. Your business plan must describe how you are going to achieve this vision.

Your goals and values will contribute to a mission statement. This statement will enable you to create a vision for the business.

Ask yourself the following questions:

- Who are the people involved in the business?
- What do they do for the business?
- How well do they do it?
- Who benefits from the solution offered by the business?
- How do you look after your team and your customers?

Look at your answers and turn the keywords into a statement of one or more sentences. Just like your personal elevator pitch from earlier in the book, make sure that it is short and concise enough to deliver at any time. Your mission statement and your vision must inspire and impress the listener. A good mission statement encapsulates your overall goals for the business.

At this stage, you will be clearer on what your business does, what it sells, and who your customer is. Again, your target market is an ideal community to ask for feedback on your product or service.

Summary

In this chapter, we learned about planning a business.

- Writing a business plan
- Branding a business
- Describing your mission and vision for your business

Next Steps?

How will you fund your business? Depending on your personal finances or circumstances, you may be self-funding or looking for a loan. Determining what your financial needs are is a critical part of your business plan.

Chapter 6:

The Business of Finance

"Empty pockets never held anyone back.
Only empty heads and empty hearts can do that."
Norman Vincent Peale

You need money to start a business.

Whether you fund your business yourself or get a loan and or investment, your personal finances will be affected. You will most likely be unable to pay yourself during the start-up stage. Many government agencies in many countries have start-up and accelerator programs where you can seek advice from existing entrepreneurs and gain mentoring and some funding.

The more you know about finance, the easier it will be to assess the viability of your business in the beginning and as you grow. This knowledge starts with your own financial decisions. Let's look at the topic of personal finance.

The Least You Need to Know

You need to develop healthy money habits and manage your personal finances. This involves balancing the following:

- Spending and Saving
- Needs and Wants
- Tracking and Budgeting
- Good habits with your personal finances will help you balance the main financial aspects of your business:
- Revenue and Expenses
- Profit and Loss

Bank Loan vs. Venture Capitalist Investment

If you don't have enough finance to fund the start-up yourself, you will need to consider a bank loan or investment from a venture capitalist or angel investor. They both have advantages and disadvantages.

A venture capitalist (VC) will invest and go on your adventure with you. They will take the risk with you, but they will need a percentage of your business for their investment. When pitching to a VC, you must convince them that you will make a healthy profit and turn their investment into a healthy return.

Your business plan must cover every aspect of the business. If the business is successful, the VC will have a share of the profits. If the business isn't successful, you don't have to pay them back as they took the risk with you. Having a comprehensive business plan will help an investor determine that level of risk and whether they want to jump in with you.

A bank needs a comprehensive business plan and a clear outline of the business. They need to see that the business model will be successful so that you can pay back your loan. A bank will charge you interest on this loan, but they will not share any of the profits of the business. However, the loan will still need to be repaid whether you are successful or not. Banks don't take risks with you!

Financial Plan

Every business needs a financial plan, even charities, and not-for-profit organizations. It will answer the following questions:

- How will you fund your business?
- What are the business expenses and costs?
- How will the business make money?
- What is the short-term financial projection?
- What is the long-term financial projection?

These projections are usually broken up into three-month sections and are referred to as quarters. You will often hear people use Q1–4 to refer to quarters.

Top Tip

Learn the language of financial statements. You may outsource the financial aspects of your business to accountants or bookkeepers, but you need to know how your business intends to make money and how it operates. You need to be able to read a Profit and Loss statement and understand your cash flow at the very least. Remember the Profit Equation: Revenue – Expenses = Profit. How does this impact the cash flow of your business? Knowing your numbers and staying on top of your financial information will help you make improvements, streamline expenses, and increase profits.

Are you getting better results from online marketing, but not print advertisements? This kind of analysis helps you save money and find your target market.

A Word on Economy

Economics of an industry, sector, country, or even the world can affect our financial decisions and behavior. Just the recent pandemic and resulting worldwide shutdown shows us that the economic outlook of our business isn't fixed or static. It is always evolving and businesses need to evolve with it.

Economics is concerned with balancing:

- Supply and Demand
- Costs, Benefits, and Incentives

Microeconomics is the role consumers and businesses play in the economy. It involves their spending and saving decisions and even what they perceive to be their needs and wants. Costs, benefits, and incentives affect consumer decisions. However, not all consumer decisions are rational. Many consumers make spending decisions based on emotion, advertising, and influence.

Macroeconomics focuses on how government and economic policies affect the decisions consumers make. If resources are scarce, a policy is generated to incentivize businesses to conserve resources and, in turn, consumers to curb spending. For instance, governments are forced to impose water restrictions in drought-prone regions. This will affect growers of crops and raise the price of their products. Think of the price of gas to fuel your car and a government incentive or tax break if you purchase an electric vehicle. This is just one example of how policies and practices can affect your business or your own spending decisions.

They are interdependent.

Key Terms

Scarcity: Limited or scarce resources for popular items, necessities, or unlimited wants.

Supply and Demand: The volume of goods that changes hands in the market.

Market price: This is the current price of goods that is affected by supply and demand.

Costs and Benefits: Maximizing the relative number of benefits to costs in their spending decisions. People make decisions based on individual benefits.

Government Economic Policy: Scarcity and limited resources drive governments to make decisions on policy to generate incentives.

Incentives: The operation of supply and demand can encourage producers to supply the goods that consumers want and or encourage consumers to conserve scarce resources. This causes the market price of goods to fluctuate.

Summary

In this chapter, we learned about financial planning to fund a business. A financial projection plan is part of a business plan.

- Bank Loan vs. Venture Capitalist
- Financial plan as part of a business plan
- Economic factors from industries and governments

Next Steps?

Effective business marketing influences our spending choices and can affect our rational balancing of needs and wants. Businesses can influence us to make certain spending choices through effective marketing.

In turn, we need to employ marketing strategies ourselves to tell future customers about our business.

Chapter 7:

The Business of Marketing

"The aim of marketing is to know and understand the customer so well that the product or service fits him and himself."

Peter Drucker

How will you promote your business? Marketing tells people about your unique solution to a real problem. Your marketing strategy must be focused and measurable. There are so many channels out there and it's best to choose a few to start with and then review how effective those options have been. Only spend money on marketing that gets results.

The Least You Need to Know

The Marketing Mix

This is a term used to describe the main elements of marketing:

- Product
- Price
- Promotion
- Place
- People

These factors interact with each other and can affect future business decisions. Marketing is not only about promotion. Your business must constantly monitor the quality of its product and the value of this product to the consumer. Is your price too high? Are you promoting it in the right markets? What kind of feedback are you hearing from your clients and customers? This is all information you need as you develop a marketing plan and adjust your plan in the future. You need to evaluate what is working and what methods are less successful. Monitoring and adapting to consumer needs and marketing channels is crucial.

In Jeff Blount's book, *People Buy You,* he emphasized that the people in the business, the people selling the product, and the people interacting with customers can influence the experience of a customer and influence future revenue. You aren't just selling a product or service. You are using those soft skills you've learned to sell your brand and yourself.

Caring about the "people" part of your business and monitoring customer satisfaction and feedback is an integral part of running a business. Good reviews and testimonials have a lot of power as a marketing tool. Negative reviews can really harm your brand. Your customers will find you through word-of-mouth from satisfied clients.

Marketing Channels

The following channels can be used to market your business:

- Email
- Newsletter
- Twitter
- Facebook
- LinkedIn
- Instagram
- Pinterest

- SMS
- Website
- Blogs/Online Communities
- Podcasts
- Media advertising
- Print advertising
- Direct Mail
- Marketing Events
- Networking
- Face-to-Face direct selling
- Phone calling

Developing Your Marketing Mix

A successful business plan will consider all of these marketing outlets and options and choose those that will have the most impact. Will you focus on word-of-mouth recommendations from customers? Would it be helpful to give incentives to return clients or bulk pricing to bigger accounts? All of these considerations are part of your marketing mix. While you may not be cold calling people on the phone, you may start a podcast or blog to reach potential customers. Let's take a look at two big marketing areas.

Website and SEO

Your website is your shop window and e-commerce is now more important than ever. To increase your market reach, you can use a tool known as search engine optimization (SEO). By using targeted keywords in your description, your business will rise to the top of internet searches. Creating blog content for your website can also drive more traffic to your website. Focusing on SEO can help your site show up on the first page of a Google search, as consumers rarely keep scrolling past the first or second page.

Networking and Marketing Events

Networking is an effective way to promote your business. It doesn't have to be a high-pressure approach where you are handing out your business card to everyone you see. Have your elevator pitch ready and give a clear message on how your business is making a change for the good. By attending marketing events, you can cultivate your network and maybe even find other entrepreneurs who will refer clients to your business.

It is wise to link in with similar professionals and potential customers on appropriate social media channels. This way you can keep in touch long after the networking event has passed. Something may trigger a reason for you to reach out again to these people to keep yourself visible in their minds. It could be an article you read, a program you watched, a movie, an interview on the radio, or something in the news.

If you have a catering business that provides food for large events, you will want to be part of a bridal fair where future brides check out potential vendors. You will most likely meet event planners and venue owners, which could lead to mutual referrals. This kind of networking is essential to build your business.

Summary

In this chapter, we learned about the different ways to tell your future customers about your business. A marketing strategy is a key part of a business plan.

- The Marketing Mix
- Marketing Channels

Next Steps?

SWOT and PEST analyses are important elements of your business plan. Entrepreneurs use these periodically to monitor and assess the internal and external influences on the business. It is always useful to re-examine your progress.

Chapter 8:

SWOT and PEST Analysis on Your Business

"It is not the strongest of the species that survives, nor the most intelligent, but the one most responsive to change."

Charles Darwin

Change is an inevitable part of any business and taking a moment to analyze your business can help you keep up with the changes. A SWOT analysis was mentioned in Chapter 1 of "You're Hired." This was a personal analysis of yourself to establish your goals and create your personal elevator pitch, telling people about you.

A SWOT analysis reveals the internal strengths and weaknesses of an organization and any external opportunities and threats it faces. It is a tool to plan realistic goals and objectives for maximum productivity while minimizing risk and any unfavorable outcomes.

A PEST analysis examines further the external factors which can affect your business. The PEST analysis has a more long-term view on the organization's potential than the more immediate SWOT analysis revelations.

Both analyses provide information so that businesses know when to pivot and change direction, reacting quickly to external factors.

The Least You Need to Know

SWOT Analysis

Answer these questions:

Strengths: What does the business do well?

Weaknesses: What could the business do better?

Opportunities: What opportunities are open to the business based on its strengths?

Threats: What external threats could harm the business based on its weaknesses?

Create a grid as you did for your personal SWOT analysis and write down as many factors as possible that relate to your business and its future.

PEST Analysis

Answer these questions:

Political: –How does current and how could future government legislation and regulation affect the business?

Economic: –How does current and how could future economic trends from home and abroad affect the business?

Social: How does current and how could future social trends and consumers' behavior affect the business?

Technology: – How does current and how could future technology capabilities and connectivity affect the business?

PEST ANALYSIS

PEST analysis helps you determine how these factors will affect the performance and activities of your business in the long term. Just list the factors that can affect your business in a grid as you did for the SWOT analysis. Here are some examples of areas you should be considering.

Political	**Economic**
Ecological/environmental issues Current home market legislation Future home market legislation International legislation Regulatory bodies and processes Government policies Government party changes Trading policies Funding, grants, and initiatives Home market lobbying/pressure groups International pressure groups Wars and conflict	Home economy situation Home economy trends Overseas economies and trends General taxation issues Taxation specific to product/services Seasonality/weather issues Market and trade cycles Specific industry factors Market routes and distribution trends Customer/end-user drivers Interest and exchange rates International trade/monetary issues
Social	**Technology**
Lifestyle trends Social demographics Consumer attitudes and opinions Media views Law changes affecting social factors Consumer buying patterns Fashion and role models Major events and influences Buying access and trends Ethnic/religious factors Advertising and publicity Ethical issues Technological Competing technology development Research funding	Maturity of technology Manufacturing maturity and capacity Information and communications Consumer buying mechanisms through technology Technology legislation Innovation potential Technology access, licensing, patents Intellectual property issues Global communications

A Word on Risk

As mentioned before, entrepreneurs are generally not risk-averse people. They "have a go" and are not afraid to fail. They realize that success is about progress, not perfection and operate in a timely fashion. Failures to entrepreneurs are opportunities to learn and be better next time.

However, entrepreneurs are acutely aware that risk is concerned with uncertainties and that any unfavorable events have outcomes and consequences.

Therefore, entrepreneurs take calculated risks where possible. They carry out SWOT and PEST analyses to make more knowledgeable and calculated risks.

They are never standing still and are ready to adapt and change due to internal and external influences at any time to maximize success. By looking at the numbers and trends in your business and industry, you will be taking calculated risks too.

Summary

In this chapter, we learned about analyzing both internal and external effects on a business at any given time.

- SWOT Analysis
- PEST Analysis
- Calculated Risk

Just as the advice that was given to me regarding this book, "done is good enough," don't overanalyze your business plan and waste time by tweaking it forever. Get out and start telling people about your business. You can do all the research and set yourself up for success, but you will make mistakes and need to adapt.

Next Steps?

Whether you're looking for funding, marketing your business, or just telling people you know about your business, you need a business elevator pitch. A brief version of this tells the listener about your business in approximately thirty seconds. Let's get ready to create the perfect pitch.

Section C:

All About You Pitching Your Business and Forming a Team

You may start off as one person wearing many hats, but success often involves creating a team as your business grows. Being a great team leader is the hallmark of any successful entrepreneur.

This is the section where you pull out a lot of the learning from "You're Hired" and "To Promotion and Beyond" as you communicate yourself and the business in a clear and confident way whether in a one-to-one situation or to a large group. Entrepreneurs rely on their full suite of soft and people skills while building, inspiring, and leading a team.

In this section, you will learn how to pitch your business to others, what makes a great team, and how to encourage people to join you on your adventure.

Chapter 9:

Pitch Your Business

"Business Development 101: Don't sell me. I'm not interested in your elevator speech. Engage me! Connect with me! And then maybe...."

Michelle Sandlin

You never know when the opportunity to speak about your business will arise. It could be at a marketing event, a chance meeting with someone in your community, or the friend of a friend. You need to be ready to evangelize about your business. You need a clear and simple message of why you started the business, what the business does, and how you do it better than anyone else. Your pitch must sell the benefits of your business.

A personal elevator pitch was covered earlier in this book. Now you are developing a powerful elevator pitch for your business. It is a short description of what you do and, if convincing enough, it will make the listener want to hear more.

Make it personal and relatable, telling the story about the change for the good. Keep sentences short and succinct, making sure it is thirty to sixty seconds long. Keep jargon out of it and leave a lasting positive impression.

Try to not start every sentence with "I" sentences. For instance, "I invented X. I can sell X, and I am the best at X." Instead, use phrases that put the customer first. One example would be "people who have used my product benefit from X."

The Least You Need to Know

Start an outline of your pitch with words and phrases. You don't need complete sentences at this stage, just bullet points. You can get into the who, what, where, when, why, and how of your business as you create your outline.

You can use the answers to the following questions to start your outline:

- Who am I?
- What do I offer?
- What problem do I solve?
- How am I different from other companies?
- What are the main contributions I can make?
- What should the listener do because of hearing this?

When you have your bullet points as an outline, you can expand on each bullet point to form sentences. Pick out the most important parts and start creating your pitch. Read it over and over until you are happy with your final pitch. Make sure it is no more than ninety words long.

To sell to customers, market your business, or secure a bank loan or funding you need a business pitch. By now, you have a mission statement for your business outlining your vision. This must be a strong and inspiring element of your pitch.

Use everyday language. Don't be tempted to be over-perfect— it might not sound as authentic.

Practice your pitch every chance you get, at meetings, with friends, at work, in fact, any time you get the opportunity. You will soon notice a difference in your confidence and be able to pivot smoothly, according to the needs of the listener, just start by networking.

Checklist Action

Read over your pitch and record yourself delivering it on your smartphone. Listen to your speech and ask yourself these questions. "What's in it for me?" is a phrase we've all heard or said. Think of the needs and wants of the person you're delivering the pitch to.

People like to hear numbers. Try to incorporate numbers into your pitch. It could be any of the following: The four products that you sell, the three reasons why you started the business, the five services that you offer people or the three benefits of your product or service. Numbers keep people engaged, but don't give them all four of these examples all at once.

You need to "get them at hello!"

- Is it short and snappy?
- Is it clear?
- Is it pleasant?
- Does it mention your name and the name of the business?
- Does it mention the problem you're solving?
- How are you making life simpler, easier, better, quicker, for your customers?
- Does it mention your USP?
- Is there a call to action at the end of the pitch?

- Is there a convincing conclusion to leave the listener wanting to hear more?

So, You Got Them at Hello?

Giving Your Next Level Pitch

The next level pitch is longer with more detail and includes measurable results and feedback from customers. The most effective way to deliver this is through PowerPoint or a similar presentation platform. It is essentially an in-depth, powerful, and inspiring version of your business plan. It tells the story of Why.

This PowerPoint presentation of your pitch needs to have enough detail to either make sales, secure funding, or secure a bank loan.

Use approximately ten to fifteen slides. Have extra slides at the end with more detail in case you're asked a specific question. Time it so that it is no longer than twenty minutes. Offer to take questions at the end so that your flow is not interrupted.

Use large font and imagery on your slides. Don't crowd your slides. Less is more!

Pictures and inspirational quotes are effective if used in moderation. A working prototype is far more powerful than a picture.

Remember your energy and confidence levels—you are entertaining as well as informing. Use animated body language and gestures to match the message you are projecting. Start strong and finish strong.

Key checklist

- Repeat the brand
- Have the business name on each slide
- Deliver your thirty-second pitch as an opener
- Recite your mission statement and vision
- Think why? Use an emotional message
- Tout the benefits—Advantages of customers buying your product or service

Your PowerPoint presentation slides need to follow a logical order and build upon the information in the previous slide. You don't want to just throw up a bunch of facts and figures without a coherent presentation that leads to a conclusion. Start by explaining the problem and then offer solutions. You can't persuade vendors or investors unless they have heard your Why.

Here is a good order of slides and information for your presentation:

1. Problem
2. Solution/USP
3. Strategy
4. Opportunity
5. Team
6. Finance
7. Why
8. Business model and proposition

9. Revenue model

10. Action

11. Thank You

12. Any Questions

Revisit the section on public speaking and presenting. Remember to resist the urge to:

- Put your hands in your pockets
- Fold your arms over your chest
- Fiddle with your hair or your face
- Clench your fists
- Mumble
- Apologize at any point
- Read every word verbatim

Summary

In this chapter, we learned about the importance of communicating what your business is and what it does clearly in approximately thirty seconds.

- A business elevator pitch conveys your mission, brand, and vision.
- Focus on the Who, What, Why, How, and Where questions.
- Along with a business plan, this pitch can be developed into a more comprehensive pitch to seek a bank loan or investment funding.

Next Steps?

You can't run a business on your own. Even if the idea for the business was your initial idea, you need to surround yourself with a team of people that you can lead. You can outsource some functions, but you can't outsource leadership and passion.

Chapter 10 provides tips on leading, inspiring, and building a dream team.

Chapter 10:

Leadership and Team Building

"Whatever words we utter should be chosen with care for people will hear them and be influenced by them for good or ill."

Buddha

Leadership and Team Building

Good leaders aren't afraid to surround themselves with people who are "better" than themselves. We aren't talking about social status or financial means. A good leader wants to hire people who are the best in their field of knowledge. Good leaders are confident enough to know that an excellent team will support a leader and the business. They want people who excel, want promotions, and aren't afraid to shine. Leaders don't need to know it all. They need to know when to delegate and surround themselves with a competent team.

To build a team, you need to encourage your team and give praise where praise is due. Remember, never expect people to do something that you would not do yourself.

Share ideas and successes with those around you. Your team will help you build upon those successes. A successful leader is acutely aware of how to influence and impact in a positive way. Never underestimate the importance of values, empathy, sincerity and flexibility, and ethics. To lead, you need to display these values. To lead you must be "on brand" at all times.

Remember your mission statement. You are your mission statement. Lead by example.

The Least You Need to Know

Successful personal attributes of a successful leader:

- Belief in yourself
- Belief in your products and services
- Belief in your future
- Optimism
- Enthusiasm and passion
- Dedication
- Perseverance and consistency

Consistent and Clear Communication

As Winston Churchill said, "The difference between leaders and mere managers is communication." Simply put, communicate clearly and often with your team. Show the team that goals tie in with the vision and mission of the company. Tell them what your expectations are. They are not mind readers. Speak their language to avoid any confusion.

Be visible, credible, and available for catch-up meetings. Good management ensures great results.

Clearly define roles and responsibilities at regular meetings. Don't be afraid to set high-performance expectations and balance this with encouragement and praise. Review performances regularly and if there's a performance problem, don't ignore it, but promptly have the conversation. Start this conversation on a positive note and let them speak.

An effective leader leads by example and demonstrates effective communication skills with both the team and any other people related to the business, like customers and suppliers. A leader's standard of communication should always be clear, consistent, and considerate.

I know a chairman and CEO who finishes all of his conversations with staff with "well done." Positivity is contagious. No matter what age we are, we all like a little praise. Showing gratitude and appreciation will boost morale and lead to better understanding and cooperation.

Optimism

An optimistic leader is future-minded and rarely displays negativity or becomes pessimistic. Optimistic leaders are mentally tough and self-determined. They show persistence and perseverance and focus on the strengths and opportunities of the team.

> **"I always like to look on the optimistic side of life, but I am realistic enough to know that life is a complex matter."**
>
> ***Walt Disney***

Summary

In this chapter we learned about inspiring a group of people to turn a business idea into a reality.

- Believe in yourself and your business idea.
- Be confident enough to hire people with the best skills for the business.
- Communicate clearly and regularly with your team.
- Be optimistic, positive, and encouraging.

Next Steps?

You should never be finished learning. Be present, enjoy working, and learn something new every day. You are well on your way to becoming a leader and working with others!

Conclusion

Thank you for reading this far.

I hope that you enjoyed reading this book. By the end of each chapter, you will have taken small steps. And we all know what happened when a few small steps were taken—a giant leap!

I hope that you download and play the board game *You're Hired.*

You can revisit any chapters and deepen your learning by reading some of the books mentioned in this book.

"The greatest investment a young person can make is in their own education, in their own mind. Because money comes and goes. Relationships come and go. But what you learn once stays with you forever."

Warren Buffet

So many people have told me that they would have loved to have read this book while in school. This book is not only for young graduates. Pass this book onto anyone who may be interested in learning these soft skills. Pass this book onto people who want others to learn these soft skills, whether it's parents and teachers of teens, university lecturers, or graduate program managers in corporate businesses.

ACKNOWLEDGEMENTS

I'd like to thank everyone who helped me with creating this book. To my first reader, my husband Paul, thank you for all your advice and support. To my launch team, thanks for your commitment and support to get the word out. To Jennifer Bradshaw, my editor, thank you for your encouragement and help to turn the book into a polished offering. To Nada and Joris at Cutting Edge who patiently designed many cover options and ultimately the final version. To everyone who gave me feedback on the book cover and title. To Tim Draper who so kindly agreed to write the Foreword to the book for me. Finally, to all my extended family and friends that have been supportive throughout the journey, you know who you are!

ABOUT THE AUTHOR

Fiona lives in Dublin, Ireland, with her husband, Paul, and sons, James and Donal.

Fiona is passionate about educating for the twenty-first century and has been empowering people from all educational levels through education, training, and mentoring. She has developed learning programs for all ages to develop and enhance their personal skills through active learning.

Fiona initially trained as an Educator in Froebel College Dublin, teaching seven- to twelve-year-olds for many years. Fiona holds a MA in Educational Leadership and Management and set up BizWorld Ireland in 2011 to bridge the gap between the business and educational community, equipping the next generation of young teenagers with the skills for entrepreneurship.

Fiona has developed Educational Programs in areas like communications, critical thinking, money management, decision making, self-awareness, empathy, team building, and innovation. Fiona particularly likes working with young adults as they prepare to make life-changing decisions around their careers.

Fiona wrote *Career Elevator* as a culmination of her extensive experience empowering people and organizations for over twenty years. Personal skills are often ignored in favor of professional skills and *Career Elevator* seeks to address that imbalance.

For more information on the programs and learning tools she offers, please visit http://www.careerelevatorbook.com

Connect with Fiona on: linkedin.com/in/fionamckeon

Review Ask

Did you find this book helpful?

Don't forget to leave a review!

I'd love to hear your thoughts on the book which will help me with future projects.

Every review matters, and it matters a *lot!*

Head over to Amazon or wherever you purchased this book to leave an honest review for me.

I thank you most sincerely.